HOW TO BE A

PERSON

HOW TO BE A
PERSON

the Stranger's  GUIDE TO COLLEGE

SEX ★ INTOXICANTS ★ TACOS

AND LIFE ITSELF

BY LINDY WEST ★ DAN SAVAGE

CHRISTOPHER FRIZZELLE ★ BETHANY JEAN CLEMENT

AND THE STAFF OF *THE STRANGER*

SASQUATCH BOOKS
SEATTLE

Printed in the United States of America

Published by Sasquatch Books
17 16 15 14 13 12   9 8 7 6 5 4 3 2 1

Cover design, interior design, illustrations, and composition
by Corianton Hale

Library of Congress Cataloging-in-Publication Data is available.

ISBN-13: 978-1-57061-778-2

Sasquatch Books
1904 Third Avenue, Suite 710
Seattle, WA 98101
(206) 467-4300
www.sasquatchbooks.com
custserv@sasquatchbooks.com

CONTENTS

PREFACE... xvii

INTRODUCTION.. xix
Just Calm Down, Don't Freak Out, All Kinds of Things Are About to
Happen to You .... **xix**

1. WHAT NO ONE ELSE WILL TELL YOU ABOUT COLLEGE................................. 1

How to Get Along With People Who Are Different from You **1**

How to Get Along With Roommates Who Are Different from You .. **3**

On Making Friends **4**

A Few Majors That You Should Not Major In...................... **5**

Everything There Is to Know About Whatever Major You Choose
(Or, Who Needs Classes?)....................................... **6**

   Physics.. **6**

   Art **6**

   Psychology **7**

   Computer Science **8**

   Theater.. **8**

   Biology.. **9**

Chemistry **10**

Classical Music **10**

Literature **11**

Economics **12**

Journalism **12**

History **13**

Philosophy **14**

What No One Else Will Tell You About Dropping Out **15**

2. A GUIDE TO AMERICA **17**

The Pacific Northwest **18**

The Midwest **19**

California **19**

The Southwest **20**

The South **21**

The Northeast **21**

The Mountains **22**

Alaska **23**

Hawaii **23**

3. WHAT NO ONE ELSE WILL TELL YOU ABOUT SEX AND DATING **25**

How to Get With a Girl If You Are a Boy **25**

How to Get With a Boy If You Are a Girl **26**

How to Get With a Gay/Lesbian If You Are a Gay/Lesbian **27**

How to Get With a Bi/Trans/Differently Sexual Person If You
Are a Bi/Trans/Differently Sexual Person **27**

How to Turn a Crush Into Something More. **28**

How to Ask Someone Out. **29**

How to Take Someone on a Romantic Date. **30**

How to Kiss **30**

How to Successfully Put Your Parts in or on Another Person. **31**

Different Sexual Positions You Need to Try in College **32**

How to Have a One-Night Stand **33**

How to Have Casual Sex. **34**

How to Be in a Relationship **35**

Honesty Actually Is the Best Policy. **35**

Cover Your Junk! How to Not Impregnate an Individual or
Get Impregnated Yourself, and, Also Very Importantly, Not
Get a Sexually Transmitted Infection (Because You Really
Don't Want That) **36**

A Little More About STIs. **37**

How to Break Up With Someone. **38**

How to Get an Abortion **39**

A Note on Polyamory. **40**

4. HOW TO BE GAY **41**

What to Do If All Your Life You Have Secretly Wanted to Have
Sex With Someone With the Same Private Parts as You. **41**

A Note About Anti-Gay Bigots **43**

How to Come Out of the Closet. **43**

Where to Go to College If You're Gay **45**

The History of Gay People in a Few Paragraphs.....................**46**

On Gay People Sleeping With Straight People **47**

How to Have Sex With a Man If You're a Man **48**

How to Have Oral Sex...**49**

How to Have Anal Sex **49**

How to Have Sex With a Woman If You're a Woman................**50**

5. HOW TO SLEEP WITH YOUR PROFESSOR 53

6. SAVAGE LOVE, COLLEGE EDITION 59

So I Have This Roommate...**59**

So I Have This Religion...**66**

So I Just Discovered Anal Sex.......................................**72**

So I've Been Thinking About Polyamory **75**

So I Have These Parents..**82**

So I Have This Kink...**86**

So I'm in This Relationship and Something About the Sex Just
Isn't Right...**97**

So I Think I Just Cheated..**100**

So I Think I Just Got Raped...**102**

So I Think I'm Pregnant...**104**

So I Think I'm Trans **106**

So I'm a Virgin—Or My Partner Is.................................**109**

7. WHAT NO ONE ELSE WILL TELL YOU ABOUT DRINKING 115

How to Deal With a Hangover 116

How to Binge Drink 118

Handy Synonyms for Being Drunk 119

On Vomiting 120

Handy Synonyms for Vomiting 121

How to Get Roofied and Still Have a Good Time 121

How to Drink Like an Adult 122

On Drinking and Driving 124

Beer: It's All Good 124

Wine: What the Hell's the Deal? 124

Why Do the Drinks at This Bar Cost So Goddamn Much? 126

8. WHAT NO ONE ELSE WILL TELL YOU ABOUT DRUGS 129

Don't Do Drugs! Okay? Seriously! Ever 129

Marijuana 131

Cocaine 132

Methamphetamine 133

Ecstasy 134

LSD 135

Mushrooms 135

Heroin **136**

A Note That Could Save Your or a Friend's Life **137**

A Final Word About Drugs **138**

9. A FEW WORDS ABOUT MANNERS 139

A Few of the Basics **139**

How to Have a Conversation **140**

How to Take a Compliment **141**

How to Be a Guest at a Party **141**

How to Host a Party **142**

On Toilets **144**

10. HOW TO DO LAUNDRY 147

How to Actually Do Laundry **151**

11. WHAT NO ONE ELSE WILL TELL YOU ABOUT FOOD 153

How to (Not) Be a Foodie **153**

So You're a Vegetarian! **157**

A Really Easy, Really Pretty, Really Good Soup You Can Make
With a Butternut Squash **157**

How to Make Tacos **158**

How to Make Very Tasty Pasta **160**

How to Make the World's Best Macaroni and Cheese
(With a Monogram on It!) **161**

How to Make an Impressive Entire Roasted Chicken **163**

Make Your Own Coffee! **165**

Organic Food: WTF? **165**

12. WHAT NO ONE ELSE WILL TELL YOU ABOUT MUSIC, BOOKS, AND ART 167

How to Be Into Music Without Annoying Everyone **167**

What the Albums in Your Dorm Room Say About You **169**

What the Art Posters in Your Dorm Room Say About You **170**

Everything You Need to Know to Successfully Flirt
With a Film Nerd **171**

Spoiler Alerts for the Big Novels So You Can Flirt With English
Nerds as If You've Already Read Them **172**

Books You Should Avoid **174**

13. WHAT NO ONE ELSE WILL TELL YOU ABOUT POLITICS 175

Getting Started **175**

How to Know If You're a Republican or a Democrat **177**

Take It Easy on Tattooing Yourself in Your Beliefs **179**

When It's Okay to Yell at Someone About Politics **179**

What No One Else Will Tell You About Feminism **182**

Guess What? You Are a Feminist **182**

First-Wave Feminism: Maybe We Could Be Citizens Now? **183**

Second-Wave Feminism: Maybe You Could Stop Raping Us,
Please? **183**

Third-Wave Feminism: Maybe I Like Rape! Shut Up! Maybe I
Don't! Shut Up! **184**

Postfeminism: Sexism Is Dead! Long Live Sexism! **185**

Stop Victim-Blaming! **185**

Stop Slut-Shaming! **185**

Gender Is a Social Construct: What ARE You!? **185**

Women Do Not Exist for the Purposes of Your Boner **186**

Male Privilege: It Is Real, and It Is Totally Bogus **186**

A Final Note: Yes, Indeed! **187**

14. SOME FINANCIAL ADVICE COURTESY OF THE BIBLE
.... **189**

Eschew Credit Cards.. **189**

Get Thee Unto a Credit Union..................................... **191**

The Bible Further Suggests That You Get a Job **191**

Jesus Christ on a Bicycle, Don't Buy a Car....................... **192**

The Golden Rule and Beer **192**

15. HOW TO USE A COMPUTER
.... **195**

Things the Internet Is Good For (Now)............................ **195**

Things the Internet Is Not Good For (Yet) **196**

Trolls Be Trollin' 196

How to Twitter 197

How NOT to Facebook 198

Sexy, Sexy Pornos!!! 198

SHOW ME YER BOOBZ 198

How to Un-Spam Thyself 199

How to Date People Inside Your Computer and Not
Get Murdered 199

16. HOW TO WRITE GOOD 201

Three Great Sentences and What Makes Them Great 202

What Not to Do 205

Don't Use Clichés 205

Don't Waste Time 206

Don't Overwrite 206

Don't Use First Person Unless You Have To 207

How to Write a College Paper 207

How to Write a Cover Letter 208

How to Write Poetry 210

17. WHAT NO ONE ELSE WILL TELL YOU ABOUT HEARTBREAK AND DEATH 211

How to Get Over a Broken Heart 212

When Someone You Love Dies 216

On Suicide 216

APPENDIX A. WHAT NO ONE ELSE WILL TELL YOU ABOUT WORKING IN RESTAURANTS......217

What It's Like Working for a Mom-and-Pop Bakery **218**

What It's Like Working for a Chain Restaurant **220**

What It's Like Working for a High-End Restaurant in London ..**222**

What It's Like Working as a Restaurant Janitor..................**225**

What It's Like Working as a Barista, an Incompetent Waitress,
a Barely Competent Cook, and at a Shady Café...................**226**

APPENDIX B. THE DIFFERENT KINDS OF PEOPLE THAT THERE ARE...**231**

People Who Choose to Correct You About the Definition
of "Hobo"..**231**

People Who Are Mean to Hoboes...................................**232**

People Who Still Have Jobs.......................................**232**

People Who Are Quietly Less Than $100 Away from Complete
Destitution **232**

People Who Secretly Have Vast Family Fortunes/Trust Funds to
Keep Them from Ever Knowing Complete Destitution, or Even
Mild Hardship..**233**

People Who Claim to Be Afraid of Clowns..........................**233**

People Who Don't Watch TV..**233**

People Who Will Just Have a Bite of Whatever You're Having ...**234**

People Who Studied Abroad in a Third-World Country **234**

People Who Are into Whimsy.......................................**234**

People Who Are White Who Call Black People "Brothas" When Talking to Other White People, as in, "A Lot of My Friends Are Brothas" **235**

People Who Are Old **235**

Old People Who Think Pigeons Are Their Best Friends **235**

Babies **236**

People Who Are Secret Hookers **236**

Recession Hookers **236**

People Who Are Pretty *and* Smart *and* Funny *and* Nice **236**

People Who Are Hot Greek Waiters **236**

People Who Smile at You on the Street **236**

People Who Don't Know How to Drink **237**

People Who Are Only Interesting When They're Drunk **237**

People Who Believe in Sasquatch **237**

People Who Don't Believe in Evolution but Love Antibiotics **238**

Wizards **238**

Russians **239**

Russian Wizards **239**

People Who Let Their Cat Walk Across Their Kitchen Cutting Board, Even Though Those Are the Same Fucking Paws That Have Been Tramping Around That Shit-Filled Cat Box and I Don't See a Kitty Foot-Washing Station Around Here, Do You? . . **239**

People Who Don't Know How to Navigate a Four-Way Stop or an Uncontrolled Intersection **239**

Animals That Are Really People Who Got Transformed by a Witch **239**

People Who Think "Hipsters" Are a Thing **240**

People Who Are Just a Down-to-Earth Guy, Who Enjoys the
Little Things in Life Like Going for Walks, Lifting Weights, or
Just Doing Whatever (LOL), Whose Friends Would Probably
Describe Him as Honest, Truthful, Loyal, Affectionate,
Compassionate, and Romanceful, and Is Looking for a Woman
Who Is That Rare Combination of Stunning on the Outside and
Beautiful on the Inside, and Most Importantly Down-to-Earth,
Enjoys the Little Things in Life, Loves Children, Animals, Has
a Passion, Laughter. I Especially Like Asians.....................**240**

People Who Try to Pretend Like They Already Knew the Story
About Jimmy Stewart Smuggling a Yeti Hand out of Nepal in
His Wife's Underpants...**240**

People Who Say, "Whole Foods? More Like Whole Paycheck!"...**241**

People Who Just Threw Up in Their Mouth a Little..............**241**

Women...**241**

American People of Irish Descent..............................**241**

People Who Are Bill Paxton....................................**242**

People Who Miss the Point.....................................**242**

People Who Don't Miss the Point...............................**242**

ACKNOWLEDGMENTS **243**

INDEX **245**

PREFACE

Every year, *The Stranger*, Seattle's only newspaper, puts out an issue of advice for college students—all the things you need to know about life that everyone else "forgot" to tell you.

This is a collection of the best advice *The Stranger* can muster (it's pretty good!). Rest assured, any errors or omissions are no one's fault except Dan Savage's. The three other co-authors of this book, who did not show this page to Dan before sending it off to the printer, apologize on his behalf.

INTRODUCTION

Just Calm Down, Don't Freak Out, All Kinds of Things Are About to Happen to You

Unless you grew up with assholes (in which case, congratulations! You escaped!), you've spent your life thus far happily sheltering under Mom and Dad's warm, clucky wings. Now, for the first time ever, you are alone. All alone. You are excited because you get to drink and bang people, but—fess up!—secretly, you are also *terrified*. You probably don't know how to do things like pay an electric bill, or do your taxes, or get an abortion, or stop crying. But stop! Stop crying. Don't freak out. You're definitely going to fuck some stuff up. At some point, you're

going to get a red envelope that's like "YOU DIDN'T PAY YOUR ELECTRIC BILL SO WE WILL MURDER YOU NOW." If that happens, you know what? You'll figure out how to pay the bill. If they shut your electricity off, you know what? The food in your refrigerator will spoil. If that happens, you know what? You can get new food. If you overdraw your bank account paying the bill so they'll turn your refrigerator back on and you can refrigerate your new food, you know what? You'll get a part-time job to make some more money. If you get fired from your job? Get another one. Flunk a class because you were working too much at your part-time job? Take it again. Yeah, it's annoying. Problems are shitty, and you don't know how to deal with problems yet. But problems have solutions. Almost nothing is as big a deal as it seems. Stop crying.

1. WHAT NO ONE ELSE WILL TELL YOU ABOUT COLLEGE

BY BETHANY JEAN CLEMENT, JONATHAN GOLOB,
JEN GRAVES, ANTHONY HECHT, BRENDAN KILEY,
CHARLES MUDEDE, AND LINDY WEST

How to Get Along With People Who Are Different from You

It's inevitable: At some point in your life, you're going to have to hang out with/work with/live in a tiny dorm room with/have sex with someone you just can't relate to. At all. Maybe they're a

Republican. Or from Germany or something. Maybe their custom license-plate holder says "BEING A PRINCESS IS A FULL-TIME JOB" (1. no, it isn't; 2. you're not one; and 3. we don't live in a monarchy anyway—or maybe you think that the president is the "head princess" of America?). People are terrible, and people are everywhere (for more information on people, see The Different Kinds of People That There Are, page 231).

So what do you do? Well, once you get started, it's surprisingly easy to pretend to like people. Think of it as a science experiment. In conversation, helpful phrases include "Ha-ha! Cool!" and "Bummer, dude." Better yet, try to find some common ground, like old Professor McGillicuddy's cra-a-a-zy mustache, or how much you both like *Jurassic Park* (because of the dinos!). The point is to get this person to think that you are awesome. It is way easier to like people who like you. After that, it's just equal parts tuning-out-boring-shit and laughing-at-ridiculous-shit. And if you can locate an ally with whom to make clandestine, hilarious eye contact, you're golden. Or, if you find yourself confined to close quarters with a person who is really and truly unbearable, here are three words for you: Head. Pho. Nes. Wait, that's one word. HEADPHONES. But seriously, headphones.

And if you're considering just following your natural instincts and being a dick to these people because they deserve it, DON'T. This behavior does nobody any good. You will get so much more done in life by being a slightly disingenuous nice person than an unremittingly honest asshole. More flies with honey, and all that. It's gross, but it's true.

How to Get Along With Roommates Who Are Different from You

Say that your college or university is located in Los Angeles, which means that it is full of orange guys with muscles and hard hair, and girls wearing those tiny shorts that say "LOOK AT MY ASSHOLE" across the buns. And also Ugg boots, and Malibu rum, and people who think a good career would be "shock jock," and business majors who wear suits every Friday and can't wait to go buy companies from nice old men and split them up and sell them for parts like Richard Gere in *Pretty Woman* before he learns the meaning of feelings. Say that you're not like these people, so you don't fit in.

In this case, not fitting in is far superior to the alternative, but that's cold comfort when you can't make a single friend and have to spend a couple years living in 100-square-foot rooms with randomly assigned strangers. Maybe the first stranger is a shaky Texan model who eats nothing but canned tuna mixed with ketchup, shares a twin bed with her shaky Texan mother whenever she comes to visit, and pulverizes large sections of the asbestos ceiling trying to hang up her totally psychedelic black-light posters, a transgression for which you are both fined $100. (Perhaps she affixes the black light itself to the wall with Scotch tape. Betcha didn't know: The sound of a black light crashing to the linoleum floor in the dead of night sounds strikingly similar to a madman crashing through the window in order to skin some freshmen.) Maybe this roommate breaks up with her faraway

Texan boyfriend and listens to "Bitter Sweet Symphony" on repeat for three days. Maybe sometimes you find her hair in your bed. You live with this person for AN ENTIRE YEAR.

Maybe the second stranger is from Bangladesh ("It's pronounced BONG-gladesh"), and she smokes two packs of Newports a day (TWO, like as in the number two), she wallpapers the entire room with Absolut vodka ads, and she only owns two videocassettes: *A League of Their Own* and *Erin Brockovich*. Over and over, she watches them. Any time of the day or night, you come home and there she is—shades shut tight against the LA sun, tucked up in bed beneath a halo of wackily revamped vodka bottles, stinking of menthol and laughing, yet again, because there's no crying in baseball (there is, as it turns out, crying in cohabitation-ball).

OH MY GOD move out! YOU CAN DO THAT! All through life, if you don't like your situation, there is ALWAYS a way to change it. Find. The. Way.

On Making Friends

It's totally stupid, but it's true: In order to make friends, you have to do stuff—stuff that you're into, with other people, like join the University Anti-Ugg Club. (Or start that club. You can be the president!)

A Few Majors That You Should Not Major In

Sociology is bogus. It's a discipline that sloppily combines bastardized versions of a number of worthy, in-depth fields of study. Unless you want to read about coal mine disasters (hard on communities, who'd have guessed?) and listen to your professor bloviate about the significance of vanity license plates, this is not for you. Political science is nowhere near as asinine, but still, just major in history and get a minor in philosophy. Speaking of philosophy, while it is not an absolute no-no (no one likes an absolutist), you should know that unless philosophy majors are very, very careful, they are pompous, annoying, and repellent to those they wish to sexually attract. Journalism: Seriously? Furthermore, hardly anyone at any still-extant newspaper has a journalism degree—they all studied things that might, like, help them write better, such as English literature, or know more things about the world, such as environmental science or microbiology or history, or they skipped college altogether and attended the School of Hard Knocks. If you would like to dismantle the patriarchy, put that lady-brain to work inside the traditional phallocentric academic structure; women's studies is great, but it's a minor, not a major. And finally, communications: This is not a real thing. Actual smart people don't even know what it means. If you want a job writing press releases, though, you're probably barking up exactly the right tree.

Everything There Is to Know About Whatever Major You Choose (Or, Who Needs Classes?)

∙∙∙

EVERYTHING YOU NEED TO KNOW ABOUT PHYSICS

If stuff is still, it doesn't like to move; if stuff is moving, it doesn't like to stop. The more stuff you're trying to move, the more you need to push it to speed it up. When you push on stuff, stuff pushes back on you. Stuff likes other stuff, from a distance at least. Stuff likes becoming more chaotic, but cannot be created or destroyed; stuff can be rearranged. (All that is Isaac Newton.) Energy, like stuff, cannot be created or destroyed, only changed from one kind to another. Energy can be stored in movement, bonds between stuff, and many other places. Changes in how energy is stored allow us do things— like bake, drive, get up tall buildings, and kill each other. (That's Sadi Carnot.) Also, stuff is energy. Stuff is a lot of energy. (That's Albert Einstein.) Compress plutonium with explosives and the atoms fission, releasing the energy stored in stuff. When the energy is released in downtown Nagasaki, you kill about 40,000 people right away and another 40,000 over time. (Thanks, Enrico Fermi!)

EVERYTHING YOU NEED TO KNOW ABOUT ART

For cave painters, what you need to know is bison. That's the subject. Next came angels with big foreheads: the Middle Ages. Then Italian Renaissance, which means that objects in the distance are painted

smaller—exactly as much smaller as your eye sees them. (This fetish for verisimilitude was the real birth of photography, even though photography wouldn't be invented for another 400 years.) Things begin to fuzz out with impressionism (the greatest glorification of poor eyesight in history), speed up with futurism (don't side with them, the fascists did) and Dada (avoid this word, because its meaning is complicated and contradictory, and it will only embarrass you). Salvador Dalí was a surrealist. Surrealists are Freudians. This means a bunch of guys with perverse fixations on women's parts. Whatever you do, never say "modern art" when you mean new art. Modern art ended in 1959. Andy Warhol: still cool.

EVERYTHING YOU NEED TO KNOW ABOUT PSYCHOLOGY

In 1856, two Europeans cursed their newly born child with the name Sigismund Schlomo Freud, a nomenclatural brutality that would have condemned the young lad to a life of psychotherapy had psychotherapy existed. Little Schlomo went on to invent it, discovering his affinity for cocaine and young Viennese women in the process. A couple of decades later, some guy made a bunch of dogs slobber when they heard a bell, which proved something important. Since then, psychology has offered self-obsessed losers new reasons to whine about how miserable they are and spawned a bad pair of Robert De Niro movies, as well as Woody Allen's entire glorious oeuvre.

EVERYTHING YOU NEED TO KNOW ABOUT COMPUTER SCIENCE

In the olden days (the 1980s), computers were for green-on-black word processing and Zork. Then someone plugged some computers into each other, and there was the internet and Zork Online. Now we have fast internet, but very little Zork at all. Things change. This is known as Moore's law—the internet is twice as fast and has half as much Zork every 18 months. At some point, you will have to decide if you want to be a computer geek or just a regular computer user. There is no third option. It's not acceptable to not know how to use computers. This is like bragging that you can't read, walk, or see. You don't have to know anything about how computers work, but you do have to know about the internet. Learn some basic HTML. Get a Mac. If you can't or won't get a Mac, for the love of god, don't use Internet Explorer. If you're paying to look at porn, you're doing it wrong.

EVERYTHING YOU NEED TO KNOW ABOUT THEATER

Oedipus accidentally fucked his mom and Sophocles got famous writing about it. Aeschylus was killed by a large bird that mistook his bald head for a stone and dropped a turtle on him from a great height. William Shakespeare was the passionate, poetic one; Ben Jonson was the cerebral, cranky one. Samuel Beckett is their poetic, cerebral, cranky heir. Bertolt Brecht was a Marxist and the exception to the following rule: Political theater is bad. Everyone talks about Antonin Artaud but nobody reads him. (Read Susan

Sontag's essay on him instead.) Constantin Stanislavsky thought actors had to "live the part," so Dustin Hoffman stayed up for two nights so he could look exhausted for *Marathon Man*. (Laurence Olivier, his costar, suggested: "Try acting—it's much easier.") David Mamet wrote about men, Caryl Churchill wrote about women, and Sarah Kane wrote about herself—in a poetic, cerebral, cranky way. (She is Beckett's heir.) Then she committed suicide. Don't ever, ever disparage new work by saying it's "derivative." Fucking *everything* is derivative. That's a cowardly criticism for people who don't have anything intelligent to say.

EVERYTHING YOU NEED TO KNOW ABOUT BIOLOGY

Evolution is everything. Don't worry about RNA, DNA, cells, phylogenies, and the rest; Mendelian genetics and evolution, combined together, are the essence of biology. Briefly: New ways of doing things (Mendel's alleles) are constantly being invented by accident—when mistakes are made during the copying of the instructions. Living things with better versions of these instructions tend to overwhelm those with poorer versions. Mendel figured out anything with more than one cell working together gets two copies of instructions for any given task. One copy can be a total loss—a scratch pad where crappy instructions can reside and not harm chances of success. Sex is about sharing alleles; if two organisms can have sex and have kids that can have sex and have kids of their own, they're a species. Species evolve, not individuals. Combine these ideas together and you have the beauty of the living world in your hands.

EVERYTHING YOU NEED TO KNOW ABOUT CHEMISTRY

Stuff is made up of different arrangements of atoms; atoms are made up of a nucleus surrounded by buzzing electrons. The outer shell always wants to be filled with eight electrons. So, any arrangement that gets you there—sodium with chloride, oxygen with two hydrogens, carbon with four chlorides—will work. This is why the periodic table has eight columns and helium (with eight outer electrons of its own) doesn't explode. Some arrangements adding up to eight shared electrons are happier than others. Chemical reactions rearrange from less stable to more stable arrangements on their own, giving off energy in the process. To make a less stable arrangement, you have to put in energy as payment. Chemistry is simply accounting: You must not gain or lose atoms at any point. Ignore the nuclear physicists on this point.

EVERYTHING YOU NEED TO KNOW ABOUT CLASSICAL MUSIC

Think of it as one note that breaks into two, and then multiplies into a universe of sound and possible instruments. Start with the monks. Their chants. Very monotone. Bach is the baroque: He turns music into an argument, lines fighting with lines. Mozart is next, using a strict form that has roots in world exploration—introduce a theme in one key, wander it around and develop it in other keys for a while, and then return home with the musical spoils of all that wandering. Then comes Beethoven and Wagner: everything bigger, louder, and longer. In the 20th and 21st centuries, starting with Stravinsky, all

rules are suspended. Even the do-re-mi scale that's the basis of Western music is broken into microtones, and the system of keys gives way to other equations and algorithms (even though 12-tone music sounds impossible, it's simple: All 12 tones of an octave must be used before any can be repeated). Mozart's period is the classical period, and thus the correct meaning of the term "classical music" is music made from about 1750 to 1820 (Mozart lived from 1756 to 1791). Therefore, saying "classical music" when you simply mean nonpopular music is the equivalent of saying "modern art" when you mean new art.

EVERYTHING YOU NEED TO KNOW ABOUT LITERATURE

English literature as it is taught in college is the story of power and class struggle. Keep that in mind and your grades will never sink below a B | . The oldest known poem in English is Caedmon's "Hymn." It's about the rise of Christianity (power) and its domination/extermination of pagan beliefs (the poor). Moving on. William Shakespeare's best play is *The Tempest* because it's about the birth of the colonial era and of great importance to postcolonial theory. (Who is Caliban? The colonial subject. Who is Prospero? The colonial master. Memorize that.) The metaphysical poets— what were their poems about? An obsession with Platonic beauty? No. The birth of existentialism in an increasingly skeptical world? No. The decline of the court as the center of political and economic power and the transition to bourgeois cosmopolitanism? That's it. See how this works? We're already at John Milton. Good guy or

bad guy? Good guy—opposed censorship and absolutism. Charles Dickens wrote about the oppression of the emerging industrial proletariat. And fog. Lots of fog. The boat in Joseph Conrad's *Heart of Darkness* is a symbol for the madness of colonial greed. Then we're in the 20th century, when realism falls out of vogue because Virginia Woolf wanted to write about her feelings. High modernism has two camps: one led by Gertrude Stein (progressive) and the other led by T. S. Eliot (reactionary). There was also Ezra Pound—but Pound leads to fascism. Postmodernism is good because it marks the death of master narratives.

EVERYTHING YOU NEED TO KNOW ABOUT ECONOMICS

Economics is a social science based on the way humans behave given limited resources. There are some simple rules: A recession is fairly bad but a depression is very bad; inflation is like cholesterol—there's normal and there's bad. Economics is a very soft science. Nobody, for instance, is sure when a recession becomes a depression. It may have happened while you were reading this sentence. Also, economists issue strong statements, but those strong statements are often followed shortly by statements of surprise. There is one thing you must know: If you want to be an economist, you must be able to read and draw graphs. You should, in fact, be graphilic. Any shortcomings having to do with graphs will disqualify you from the profession, which is based entirely on graphs.

EVERYTHING YOU NEED TO KNOW ABOUT JOURNALISM

Gatekeepers have tried to erect all kinds of academic barriers to

entry into the journalism world. They say you need undergraduate journalism training, that you need graduate journalism schooling, that you need to have been editor of your school newspaper. But really, the job is not a whole lot more complicated than being able to think, write, and ask pointed questions. If you can do all of that already, and if you have something better to do than enroll in Journalism 101 or communications or whatever your school calls it, do it. Spend your college years immersing yourself in something that could actually help inform your perspective as a journalist later on. Take a couple languages. Read the great American writers—Mark Twain and Ernest Hemingway began their careers as journalists. Drink with the campus politicos. Learn about economics and statistics (the realms in which journalists are constantly being bamboozled). Learn about history. And while you're at it, start a blog and do some good writing for a school publication, preferably the campus newspaper. That way you'll be able to convince the gatekeepers that you know what you're doing when you apply for your first summer internship.

EVERYTHING YOU NEED TO KNOW ABOUT HISTORY

History is a very tricky matter these days. In the olden days, you began history with ancient Egypt and ended with post–World War II America. Not anymore. History is now fluid and complex. It's not about one group/society/state and one development, but many movements over many periods of time. There is a history for women, a people's history, a history for Asians, Africans, South Americans, Europeans, Indians, and so on. And one history is not better than

the others. Even Western history has become a complicated matter. For example, we no longer think about ancient Greeks and their highest achievement, democracy, without thinking about the huge slave population that supported that society. As for the Dark Ages, whose Dark Ages do you mean? It certainly was not the Dark Ages for the Arabs, whose civilization was thriving at the time—from Baghdad to Spain. So, when you study history at the college level, expect lots of diversity and no teleology. The history taught in the 21st century has no goal or meaning. Keep that in your head, and your grades will not sink.

EVERYTHING YOU NEED TO KNOW ABOUT PHILOSOPHY

Western philosophy begins around 500 BCE with Thales, who believed water was everything; Heraclitus, who believed change was everything; and Parmenides, who believed nothing changed. Athens' golden age came around 400 BCE, with Socrates, Plato, and Aristotle as its primary figures. What you need to know: Socrates was killed by the city of Athens because he asked too many bothersome questions and seduced too many young men; Plato, Socrates' student, hated Athens for killing his teacher (his philosophy is nothing but an expression of this hate); and Aristotle, a student of Plato, was almost killed by Athens but got out of town just in time ("I will not allow the Athenians to sin twice against philosophy," Aristotle said as he ran from the city with his belongings). As for the Romans, they did not philosophize. The next important period for philosophy is the 13th century with the

scholastics—all they could think about was Aristotle. After the scholastics, we leap to the end of the 18th century and enter what we now call German idealism (from Kant to Marx). After German idealism, there's Heidegger—he became a Nazi. After Heidegger, there are the French Nietzscheans. After their work (mostly produced around 1968), the story of speculative philosophy comes to an end. That's all, folks.

What No One Else Will Tell You About Dropping Out

The American university system is the best in the world, and it's in crisis. The economy is squeezing foundations, enrollments are increasingly difficult to predict, and the universities are responding by doing what all big, clunky institutions do when faced with a crisis: forgetting their true function and doing whatever they can to stay alive with tuition hikes, program cuts, etc. (Note to universities, newspapers, and other institutions that are having trouble keeping up with the times: Sometimes the biggest favor you can do your discipline is to disband. It hurts, yes, but you exist to further human potential and knowledge, not vice versa.)

Also, because of a demographic trend that began with the GI Bill in 1944, universities are flooded with middle-class kids who don't belong there. They don't care about learning—they're just taking up space for four to six years, waiting for a diploma, deluded into thinking it will guarantee them lives much like their parents'. If you

are one of these people, DROP OUT NOW. For two reasons: First, according to a great many economists, you will be the first of several coming generations that will be poorer than the generations that preceded you. The old models of college/work/retirement-at-65 are dead. You'll have to find a new way. Second, you're fucking it up for all the poor kids (or just-poor-enough kids who can't afford tuition but don't qualify for free rides) who deserve to be where you are.

Your hanging around college like a cow waiting for the slaughter isn't doing you any favors, it isn't doing your peers any favors, and it's not doing the university system any favors (because you're helping it keep up a false delusion about its role and relationship to society and economy). Instead, figure out what you want to do with your life and get an internship (if it's in a political or creative field) or an apprenticeship (if it's in a mechanical field). The secret to life is merely to cultivate a passion for something—anything— and follow it. That will serve you much better in the coming years.

And now, the obligatory list of famous and successful dropouts: Bill Gates, Steve Jobs, Maya Angelou, Harry Truman, Albert Einstein, Lady Gaga, David Geffen, George Orwell, Patti Smith, Wolfgang Puck, Mark Twain, William Safire, and, um, Britney Spears.

2. A GUIDE TO AMERICA

BY LINDY WEST

S o, you're a big shot now. A great big big shot, with plans and dreams and wanderlust and gas money. Look at you! Going places! Maybe you're moving away for college, maybe you're relocating for a job, maybe you're throwing a dart at a map just for the dick of it. But where are you going to go? What are you going to do? What are you going to wear? What are you going to eat? Who are you going to bang? THE UNITED STATES HAS SO MANY PLACES IN IT, YOU GUYS. Here's a little guide to help you get oriented, have fun, and fit in with the locals so you don't end up dismembered in a quarry because you used the wrong fork or something. Mind your forks.

The Pacific Northwest

. . . .

MASCOT: A dude named Jeff (he has a band).

MOTTO: "Hey, you should check out my band."

MAIN ATTRACTIONS: Kurt Cobain's house (Seattle), Bruce Lee's grave (Seattle), Crater Lake (Oregon), Space Needle (Seattle), whales (the ocean), that one vegan place with the kale chips (Portland).

This is that damp, green place up in the corner. The Pacific Northwest is the nation's leading exporter of trees, airplanes, vegans, software, serial killers, suicide bridges, polar fleece, octopus attacks, coffee-related smugness, bands, sad white people, sad white people in bands, and owls. All the stereotypes about the Pacific Northwest are both true and untrue. You will hear that it rains a lot—it does, but it rains more in Miami. You will hear that the people are passive-aggressive and cold—some are, but others aren't, because THAT'S HOW PEOPLE WORK. You will hear that everyone is always drinking a latte—FALSE, nobody drinks lattes. Normal people drink Americanos. You will hear that Washington and Oregon are both run by puppet governments controlled by Sasquatch. Yeah, that's actually true. Oregon has no sales tax. Washington has Dave Matthews. The eastern halves of both states are exact replicas of Wyoming.

The Midwest

MASCOT: A clogged artery.

MOTTO: "Ow, my artery!"

MAIN ATTRACTIONS: The Sears Tower (Chicago), the Gateway Arch (Saint Louis), the Rock and Roll Hall of Fame (Cleveland), Oprah (OPRAH!!!!!), corn (everywhere).

The Midwest is a wholesome place where everyone is nice, even the bad people (and there are several!). The sizable Scandinavian population keeps things Lutheran and bland. A typical Midwestern meal consists of feeding a cow potatoes and ham custard until it dies, then cutting the cow into steaks, stuffing the steaks with Jell-O salad, deep-frying the stuffed steaks, piling the steaks into a large mound or berm, smothering the whole thing with maple beer cheese gravy, and serving it all with a side of popcorn shrimp and "broccoli" (which is just sticks of butter carved into the shape of broccoli). Vegetables are outlawed. And for dessert: hugs!

California

MASCOT: Tom Hanks.

MOTTO: "You're fat!"

MAIN ATTRACTIONS: The Hollywood sign (Los Angeles), Yosemite National Park (Central California), the Golden Gate Bridge (San Francisco), the Integratron (Joshua Tree), gays (San Francisco).

Los Angeles is where entertainment comes from. Northern California is a utopia of breezy marijuana fields and comically large trees. Southern California is Mexico with breast implants. The rest of California is flat and covered in cow poop. All of your favorite people live in California (Weird Al Yankovic, Joan Rivers, Snoop Dogg), but all of your least favorite people live in California too (Charlie Sheen, Paris Hilton, the ghost of Ronald Reagan).

The Southwest

MASCOT: Sand.

MOTTO: "World's Greatest Grandpa."

MAIN ATTRACTIONS: Area 51 (Nevada), the Grand Canyon (Arizona), Las Vegas (Nevada).

In the bottom-left part of the country, there is a big desert where tarantulas and crazy sand-sheep lived in peace with the indigenous human population for many billions of centuries. Then one day an invading army of old people ran a garden hose all the way from California and turned the desert into a ludicrously unsustainable golf course, and all the tarantulas were like, "Whaaaaaaaat!?" and California was like, "I'm thirsty, bro!" New Mexico is like Arizona but with more hippies. Arizona is like New Mexico but with more old people and racism. Nevada is like Arizona but more prostitutey. Utah is like a church basement but with better national parks. New Mexico is like Mexico but newer.

The South

MASCOT: Delta Burke being chased by an alligator.

MOTTO: "We don't take kindly to mottos."

MAIN ATTRACTIONS: Civil War battlefields, Appalachian Mountains.

Okay, okay, so the South has had some public image problems over the years (rhymes with "blavery"—whoops!), but Americans are nothing if not forgetful. And the South really does have a lot going for it. First of all, SEERSUCKER SUITS. Second of all, BARBECUE. Third of all, SEXY VAMPIRES!!! The South might not be the number-one *easiest* place to move if you're a non-straight or a non-white or a non-vampire-hunter, but it's the 21st century and things are loosening up. Try big cities (Atlanta, Houston) and university towns (Austin, Chapel Hill), which tend to be more liberal. And full of vampires.

The Northeast

MASCOT: Ben Affleck.

MOTTO: "Wheeyad yoo fahkin' PAHK the CAH!?"

MAIN ATTRACTIONS: The Statue of Liberty (New York), Walden Pond (Massachusetts), Irish pubs (fucking everywhere), lobsters (watching you while you sleep).

Vermont and New Hampshire are exactly the same, except that part of New Hampshire is a suburb of Boston, whereas all of

Vermont is a village. Rhode Island exists so that Massachusetts can feel better about itself. Every state north of Massachusetts is where they wear flannel and talk slower. Connecticut is "more than just an extension of New York, damn it! We also have several hills and fences made out of stone!" Maine is a vast, unconquered territory of pine trees and bogs. New York thinks it's better than you, and it's kind of right.

The Mountains

MASCOT: Ted Kaczynski.

MOTTO: "Get off my land!"

MAIN ATTRACTIONS: Snow, sky, geysers, Testicle Festival (Montana).

The mountains are where people go when they don't want to be bothered. So QUIT BOTHERING THEM. Colorado is full of great skiing and creepy Christians. Wyoming is whatever Wyoming is. North Dakota is flat and brown. South Dakota is beautiful and full of bikers. Don Johnson lives in Colorado. Huey Lewis lives in Montana. Literally nobody lives in Idaho. People look to the mountain states to fulfill their idealistic dreams of the classic American West—but, of course, that dream doesn't exist anymore, having been replaced by the classic American meth. Stay away from meth.

Alaska

MASCOT: A bear, eating you.

MOTTO: "Canada's hat."

MAIN ATTRACTIONS: Bears (eating you), wolves (eating you), nature (eating you).

Alaska, at different times of the year, features both 24 hours of sunlight AND 24 hours of darkness (pick your hell!). There's tundra (actual tundra!) swarming with man-eating monsters, plus cities (not actual cities!) swarming with batshit right-wing separatists. Men grow woolly beards to keep their faces warm, and moose outnumber women 3:1. You can see Russia from there. The state bird is a cruise ship filled with fat people.

Hawaii

MASCOT: A Hawaiian person laughing at everyone who doesn't live in Hawaii.

MOTTO: "WHY THE FUCK DON'T YOU LIVE HERE!?"

MAIN ATTRACTIONS: Hawaii (Hawaii).

Hawaii is a bunch of laid-back, chilled-out volcanoes sticking out of the ocean, covered with beautiful sun-roasted people who just want to eat macaroni salad and have a good time, maaaaaan. White people did horrible, violent things to Hawaii, but Hawaii still lets white people live there, because that's just the kind of cool

dude Hawaii is. Hawaii runs on "island time," which means that all your shit is going to be fucking late. Because it's island time! Cute! Island time! Oh, also people in Hawaii looooooove huffing glue (I saw a documentary about it). The only thing they love more than huffing glue is surfing. Good times. *Island* times.

3. WHAT NO ONE ELSE WILL TELL YOU ABOUT SEX AND DATING

BY BETHANY JEAN CLEMENT, PAUL CONSTANT, CHRISTOPHER FRIZZELLE, CIENNA MADRID, AND LINDY WEST

How to Get With a Girl If You Are a Boy

ere's the main thing: Don't be creepy. Girls can smell your weird, insecure, predatory creepin' from a mile away (hint: It smells like DiGiorno and Axe body spray!). Groom yourself, don't try too hard, don't use pick-up lines, don't stare, and try to

visibly have fun. People (women are people!) like to be around people who are fun. Don't be too aggressive, but don't be too timid. Most importantly, talk to women like they are humans with interests and lives and things to say, not just fleshy collections of holes that you would like to put your penis into. Oh, and please don't wear sandals. No one wants to look at your weird toes.

How to Get With a Boy If You Are a Girl

First of all, how high are your standards? Do you exist? A lot of men will sleep with you based solely on that. Unfortunately, many of those men are hoboes. If you're trying to bag some landed gentry (or at least a renter), here's what's up: Put on some makeup (not too much). Show some skin (not too much). Find someone who can consistently cut your hair in a flattering way. Before you go out, listen to the dirtiest rap music you can find. Leave the house. Smile a lot. Convince yourself that if you were a man, you would definitely want to have sex with you. Believe it. Then project that confidence. Don't be annoying. Don't be desperate. Say interesting things but don't pander. Have fun. Congrats! Penis in vagina!

How to Get With a Gay/Lesbian If You Are a Gay/Lesbian

Oh, it's all the same as for the straights—have good hygiene, be an interesting person, don't talk with your mouth full. The key difference for gay people is that you have to come out of the closet before anything else: People who are out are much healthier and happier (and thus more datable) than people who are closeted. If you're a gay man, being in the closet will force you into a never-ending spiral of secrecy and stress and sex in bathrooms. If you're a lesbian, you'll have the spiral of secrecy and stress without the sex in bathrooms. For the love of god, come out of the closet already (if you're struggling with this, see How to Come Out of the Closet, page 43), make an account on a gay dating site, join a club or get a hobby that will force you to interact with other gay peers, and if you're old enough, hit the bars. The gay rights movement started in a bar, after all (see The History of Gay People in a Few Paragraphs, page 46).

How to Get With a Bi/Trans/ Differently Sexual Person If You Are a Bi/Trans/Differently Sexual Person

Again, it's all the same as for the straights—have good hygiene, be an interesting person, don't talk with your mouth full—but out of

the closet! (If you're struggling with this, see So I Think I'm Trans, page 106!) Be honest about who you are and what you're into, join (or start!) a club for people like you, and get online to find other likewise-sexual individuals. Also, you're awesome—don't let anyone make you feel marginalized or otherwise less-than-awesome.

How to Turn a Crush Into Something More

Gather some information about your crush without being stalker-y. What are they into? Where do they hang out? Meanwhile—and this is key—do interesting stuff yourself. Make weird art, go to see music, join some not-too-freaky political cause, skinny-dip in fountains, walk across the entire city. And books! Read books. Voilà: You're a person with unusual and fascinating experiences and observations, and that's hot. Now wrest control of your own mind: You are not hopelessly crushed out on this person who is so, so great—rather, you are a great, great person who would like to assess whether this person is a good fit for you (for whatever purposes you've got in mind). Say, "Hi, I'm [your name here]," and ask a pertinent (and ideally funny) question. Be ready to talk about what you've been up to and why it's been crazy, amazing, etc. Smile and make eye contact (this is not rocket science, people). Meanwhile—and this is key—let go of any hopes or expectations about the outcome. Think of this person as a possible friend, if—IF!—they seem cool. (It's good to test all this out on people other than your crush—people

with whom you really don't care about the outcome—frequently.) Are they responding well? Have a friendly invitation ready (see How to Ask Someone Out below), and have fun. Note: If at first you don't succeed, fuck it! Do not feel awkward or bad. Say hi next time you see them, and start looking for your next crush. At this rate, you're going to get laid—and make collateral friends along the way—at a nearly alarming rate.

How to Ask Someone Out

When you're trying to "seal the deal" with a "fly mammy" or a "drunk guy walking past your apartment," it's a good idea to have a list of super-alluring catchphrases in your back pocket (keep yours laminated for maritime seductions). Stuff like "Guess what? I'm about to blow your mind." And "Hold still while I put *this* in *there*." And "Don't look doooooooown (because I'm fingering you)!" That way, whoever you're trying to put it in knows you're a classy, serious lover who is not to be kept waiting. And also that you will finger on the first date.

Just kidding. Have you tried "Hey, would you like to hang out sometime?" Or "Do you want to go see this band/movie/weird bug that looks really great?" Because that would be a good place to start.

How to Take Someone on a Romantic Date

Yay! Good idea! How cute of you! There are a lot of ways to go about this, but the main thing is: Be thoughtful. Pay attention to what the other person likes. Are they a vegetarian? Did they mention wanting to try a particular restaurant? Did they tell you that Vietnamese food gives them diarrhea-hives? Try to avoid restaurants that will give your beloved or hopefully-beloved-to-be diarrhea-hives. Diarrhea-hives are not romantic. Tell your date they look pretty/handsome. Don't be boring. Ask questions. Candles are nice. Flowers aren't necessary but HOLY SHIT ARE THEY EXCITING. Cooking at home (see What No One Else Will Tell You About Food, page 153) isn't necessary but HOLY FUCK IS IT ADORABLE. The idea here is to make the other person feel special, so just treat the other person like they are special (not special like Special Olympics—come on) and you win. Oh, and kiss your special person. KISS THEM. KISS THEM SO MUCH.

How to Kiss

Start slow. You don't even have to open your mouth yet. Did you know that? Just put your lips against the other person's lips. Good job! Do it again! Do it slower. Smile. Cute, right? Okay, now. Part your lips a little bit. Breathe through your nose (you brushed your teeth, didn't you!? GO BRUSH YOUR TEETH) and gently touch your tongue to

the other person's tongue. The other person, hopefully, will be doing the same thing. Try to minimize saliva. Pull back. Start again. See what feels good. You can bite a person's lip a little (that's A LITTLE) if you want. You can take a person's face in your hands. Just follow your instincts. It's all about empathy here (all of sex is, really)—do you want a weird, hard tongue flicking in and out of your mouth at a rapid rate like a Komodo dragon advancing on a goat carcass? No? Do you want someone else's tongue shoved forcibly and wholly into your mouth like a gross carnivorous cave-slug? No???? THEN DON'T DO THAT TO SOMEBODY ELSE, KOMODO SLUG-MOUTH. Kissing doesn't have to be gross, but it really, really can be. Don't be part of the problem. Don't be a slug-mouth.

How to Successfully Put Your Parts in or on Another Person

Communication is important. Unless you're having sex with one of those (annoying) people who doesn't like to talk specifics because it ruins the "moment" or the "mystery," just go ahead and ASK. What do they like? What gives them the carnal tingles? What gets them off? Listen to what they say, and tell them what you want, too. Then, whatever you talked about, both of you do that with your genitals. Bingo! If you are a shy flower who just wants to DO dirty things without having to TALK about dirty things, pay close attention to your partner's body language and vocalizations. If they start making a noise like they like something, do more of that thing.

If they fall asleep, you're fired. To sum up: friction, repetition, enthusiasm, repeat. No teeth.

Different Sexual Positions You Need to Try in College

Most sexual positions apply to all genders and orientations—thus we have chosen the gender-neutral names "Pat" and "Sam" to describe our sex-position test subjects. **MISSIONARY:** Pat lies on back with legs up. Sam lies on top of Pat. **THE STOPPERAGE:** Same as Missionary, but Pat's knees are doubling as Sam's earmuffs. **DOGGY-STYLE:** Pat is on hands and knees, Sam is behind Pat, penetrating like there's no tomorrow. **SPOONING:** Pat lies down, Sam also lies down, penetrates Pat from behind. The inclusion of actual spoons is optional. **COWBOY/COWGIRL:** Sam lies down faceup. Pat climbs on top facing Sam and bounces up and down while trying to not make a joke about Native Americans. **REVERSE COWBOY/COWGIRL:** Sam lies down faceup. Pat climbs on top facing away from Sam. Both climax while secretly fantasizing about a young, hot John Wayne. **THE STEVE JOBS:** Sam stands up, idly fingering an iPod and ignoring everyone else in the room while Pat licks Sam's asshole to climax. **THE ROCK LOBSTER:** Pat hums B-52s songs at a very low volume while barely tolerating whatever Sam's doing. **THE L. RON:** Pat squats on an ottoman while reflecting on childhood traumas. Sam quickly fucks Pat from behind and then takes all of Pat's money. **REAP THE WHIRLWIND:** Sam is tied to

a chandelier. Pat is on a trampoline. Whatever penetration occurs is considered "fair game." **THE MINTZ-PLASSE GAMBIT**: Pat has one leg up on a stepladder while wearing a powdered wig. Sam leans over backward in an arch and makes a gibbering noise as they rub their jam-smeared genitals together. **THE WANDERING MISSIONARY**: Sam arrives at Pat's door wearing a short-sleeved shirt, a tie, and magical underpants. Pat fists Sam back to reality.

How to Have a One-Night Stand

Okay. You just saw this person naked, and they saw you naked. Both of you are vulnerable right now. But even though you are vulnerable, don't pull some lame backlash shit. This person just had sex with you! That was so nice of them! First of all, don't sneak out. If you don't want to spend the night, that's okay, but be kind and direct about it. If you don't want the other person to spend the night, then don't invite the other person over to your goddamn house, because there is no non-shitty way to kick someone out after you just fucked them. Sorry. Also, don't get anyone's hopes up. Don't be all, "I am totally into you and let's date! I'll totally call you in five minutes!" Because you know you're not going to do that. But also don't be a dick. Don't be all, "Get out of my house, skank! You're gross!" Try this: "Hey, I had fun! Thanks! Maybe I'll see you around sometime!" Also, eating a breakfast sandwich with a person is a nice gesture. Just saying.

How to Have Casual Sex

I know you think you want to have casual sex, but you might be wrong (I'm looking at you, vagina-havers). A lot of things will happen to you when you start sleeping around. First of all, make no mistake, sleeping around is really, really fun. Sex is fun. Meeting new people is fun. You can learn how to be good at sex—how to make yourself feel good and make other people feel good. And making other people feel good FEELS REALLY GOOD. And who knows—you might accidentally turn a casual sex partner into a full-on black-tie tux-and-tails sex partner.

That said, sometimes there's nothing more lonely than waking up in bed wrapped in a total stranger. You might get your feelings hurt (why are you good enough to fuck but not good enough to date?). You may feel guilty (stop it!). You may get hopelessly attached to a complete goober (especially if you're a female, because females have more of this stupid hormone called oxytocin that makes them get love-feelings for anyone who gives them an orgasm, so WATCH OUT).

But all that big dumb pain—it's kind of worth it. It hardens you in the right places and softens you up in others. It teaches you what you want. It's what being young and dumb and growing up is all about. So just check in with yourself. Check in with your friends. Make sure you're humping strangers for the right reasons—having fun, not self-destructing—and don't push yourself outside your comfort zone. Use a condom.

How to Be in a Relationship

Don't lose yourself. This other person likes you because you are a person, not because you are some weird, mushy, vestigial tail that they have to drag around. BE A PERSON. Hang out with your friends (your friends miss you!). Maintain your interests. Don't be afraid of space—space makes growth possible. On the flip side, remember that it's not all about you. Don't be selfish. Your partner wasn't put on this earth to make you happy—your *vibrator* was. Or your lubricated vagina-tube. Or Reese's Peanut Butter Cups. Or WHATEVER. Your partner, on the other hand, is a person, not an object. You are a person, not an object. Act like one. Take care of each other. Be nice.

Honesty Actually Is the Best Policy

College is a fine time to experiment with, say, having two boyfriends, or two girlfriends, or one of each at the same time, and maybe you're reading some Anaïs Nin and it seems extra-exciting to not let them know about each other. Yep, you're totally *a spy in the house of love*. But pretty soon you'll see that someone's feelings are going to get hurt, or that it's just exhausting and kind of stupid. In matters of love—in all matters, of everything—honesty really is the best policy. It sounds hokey, but the more honest you are about who you are and what you want, the more interesting your life is going to be.

Cover Your Junk! How to Not Impregnate an Individual or Get Impregnated Yourself, and, Also Very Importantly, Not Get a Sexually Transmitted Infection (Because You Really Don't Want That)

OPTION 1: Condoms, condoms, condoms! Condoms are so great. Basically, men wear them on their penises during sex (not all day, guys!) so that spermy things and infectiony things can't swim all up into your vagina or your man-parts! The anti-infectiony part of the condom usage also works for man-on-man stuff pretty well! Great, right? Use them. It's worth it! Because fucking rules and diseases drool! Literally! Out of your penis!

OPTION 2: Female condom. Hahahahaahahahaha!!!!! Do you like your vagina but wish it were more like a wadded-up plastic bag? Meet female condom! You know how sometimes clowns will wear those comically big pants with a Hula-Hoop for a waistband? The female condom is like that—like a one-legged Hula-Hoop clown pant. For your vagina. Hahahahaahahahahaa.

OPTION 3: The pill! Also for the ladies! Some lady-people find that the pill kills their sex drive. Some lady-people get acne. Some lady-people get PMS-style weeping and stuff every damn day when they take the pill. Some lady-people have no side effects and love the pill! And it is really good at keeping you from getting knocked up!

(Important note: It is really NOT good, AT ALL, at keeping you from getting STIs! Please see Option 1!) The only way to find out for yourself is to try, and then maybe try a different kind of pill too. Isn't it fun being a lady-person!? (Answer: Not in this case, but these kinds of problems are less problematic than certain other problems—see How to Get an Abortion, page 39.)

OPTION 4: IUD/NuvaRing/etc. ALSO for the ladies! See about the fun part!? There are a bunch of different things that can be implanted into your lady-area (or your arm! THE FUTURE IS NOW!) to intercept babies. (Important note again: These things are really NOT good, AT ALL, at keeping you from getting STIs! Please see Option 1!) Much like the pill, different products make different lady-people react differently. See what works for you, while consulting your doctor as needed.

OPTION 5: Abstinence. Ha-ha, nerd!!! (JK, abstinence is a totally valid choice, and don't let anyone make you feel ashamed of being a virgin. People can be assholes. But if you change your mind, which you probably will, see Option 1—safety first!)

A Little More About STIs
· ·

You assume all these people you want to fuck are healthy because they're young and hot, they smile a bunch (diseased people don't smile), or they've got taut asses with "Juicy" stamped across the cheeks. But even people with juicy asses can be cesspools of disease. According to a 2007 Stanford University study, one in four

college students has a sexually transmitted infection. The most common STIs on college campuses are genital warts (HPV) and chlamydia. Symptoms for chlamydia are often mild or absent, so it goes undiagnosed. Therefore, don't take someone's word that they're clean. Kiss them, fuck them, but use condoms. Condoms are the only way to reliably protect against STIs. If you begin seeing someone exclusively and want to stop using condoms, get tested first—both you and your partner. If you experience burning around your genitals, itching, a rash, pain while urinating, discharge, fever, madness, or sterility, go to the damn doctor. You probably already have an STI. Seriously. Just go. DOCTORS ARE NOT SCARY. The waiting and wondering and possibly infecting other people is the scary part.

How to Break Up With Someone

You MUST do it in person. No phone, no texting, no e-mail. You must be firm, direct, and simple. Do not leave room for argument or ambiguity or false hopes. Don't be cruel or insulting, even if you feel like it—it just makes you look bad and gives the dumpee ammunition for later. Leave as soon as you're done, and delete that person from your phone and your Facebook so you don't do anything you regret while drunk.

How to Get an Abortion

Calm down. Take a deep breath. It's going to be okay. If you are pregnant but you don't want to be, there are sooooo many options for you! Fun! Let's do this! First, make an appointment at a clinic in your area. Make sure it isn't a creepy Christian "pregnancy center," because they will just feed you a bunch of lies about your soul dying and your uterus falling out, and then send you home with some Jesus pamphlets and no abortion. Not. Fucking. Helpful. Planned Parenthood is a good place to start. Or, if you have a doctor you're already comfortable with, they can probably refer you to a good place. Be honest and ask for what you need.

The people at the clinic (almost certainly women) have met many people like you before, and they are trained in just the right ways to be nice to you and help you to stop freaking out. They will sit you down and talk to you about your feelings and your options. You will have the choice of either a medical abortion (pills that cause the unwanted clump of cells—it is not a baby—to detach and fall out) or a surgical abortion (sedation and a vacuum-type apparatus). The medical kind, where you take the pills, is easier, but either is totally fine. To repeat: You will be FINE.

People might tell you all kinds of things about your abortion: They might tell you that you are a bad person. They might tell you that you'll be traumatized for the rest of your life. They might tell you it'll be horribly painful. They might tell you that chunks of tissue the size of lemons will fall out of your vagina. Of course, everyone

is different and everyone's abortion is different (like a snowflake!), but in general, the reality is that YOU WILL BE FINE. Your heart will recover. Lemons will not come out. No lemons. If lemons come out, call the doctor, and THEN you will be fine. And if you are a bad person, it is not because of your abortion.

Lastly, congrats! You now have carte blanche to make abortion jokes for the rest of time. Use this power wisely.

A Note on Polyamory

Oh boy! See So I've Been Thinking About Polyamory, page 75.

4. HOW TO BE GAY

BY CHRISTOPHER FRIZZELLE
AND MADELINE MACOMBER

What to Do If All Your Life You Have Secretly Wanted to Have Sex With Someone With the Same Private Parts as You

Y ou have this really big secret that you've spent years hiding (not easy—congrats!). You're religious, or your parents are religious, or your best friend has a thing against gay people, or you're not wild about the gay characters you've seen on TV, or you just have the very common desire to be "normal" and the idea

of other people talking about how you're "different" makes you want to die.

That feeling that you have in your chest is your heart telling you that it's time to come clean, but your head is trying to stop that from happening, because what if . . . [*insert horrible thing that someone could say or do to you*]. That thing you're trying to stop from happening is called *coming out*, and it's super important, for at least three reasons:

1. Being gay is not something you can change. It's not something you chose. It's like being brown-eyed. You can pretend to have blue-colored eyes with those blue-colored contact lenses, but those don't fool anyone, and the sooner you get over trying to fool people, the sooner you can start to have a happy life.

2. People who are "against" gay people are fucking idiots, and often secretly gay (or curious about experimenting) themselves—in other words, hypocrites—and the last thing you should be doing is molding your life to make idiots and hypocrites happy. Idiots and hypocrites may try to convince you that being gay is "wrong" or "disgusting" or means you'll "burn in hell forever," but those people are undereducated religious fundamentalists who believe evolution is a sham and dinosaurs are a liberal conspiracy. You should relish the chance to flip these morons the finger.

3. Statistically, the people most scared of gay people are the people who don't know any gay people. The more those people realize their neighbors, brothers, moms, roommates, cousins, nieces, coworkers, veterinarians, and mailmen are gay, the less scared they'll be. By

coming out, you're doing a great favor to all the other gay people out there who don't fit the stereotype either. Keeping quiet only helps the assholes who want to stereotype and marginalize gay people because it serves their own twisted purposes. Don't let them get away with it.

A Note About Anti-Gay Bigots

Studies have shown that anti-gay people often turn out to have secret gay desires themselves. It shouldn't come as a surprise, since the psychology is so simple: They hate themselves, and they don't want this thing they hate about themselves to be discovered. If this is news to you, Google "gay sex scandal" plus "Larry Craig" or "Bob Allen" or "George Rekers" or "Ted Haggard" or "Catholic priest."

How to Come Out of the Closet

You might want to do it while driving. After all, if you're reading this, it probably means you haven't come out yet, and if you haven't come out yet, it probably means you're having a hard time imagining looking into someone's eyes and saying, "I'm gay," and the great advantage of doing it while driving is that you have to keep your eyes on the road.

Or the other person does, if they're driving.

And then it's out there.

You're done.

You don't have to do anything else.

The other person's response is their business, and it will depend entirely on them. If you are coming out to your mother and she is religious and quaint and easily fooled, she might be floored, might be hysterical, and may even start to hyperventilate. She may demand you pull the car over and let her drive, even though you're on the freeway. Since hyperventilation and the safe stewardship of a moving vehicle are incompatible, you are fully in the right to deny her request, and by the time you are off the freeway she will have collected herself (true story).

Your friends, if they are good people, will say, "I'm so glad you told me. I just want you to be happy."

If your friends are of the slightly annoying variety, they will say, "Why'd it take you so long?" or "I knew before *you* did." Don't be offended—this friend of yours is just trying to get over the offense of not being trusted with this information sooner. The human urge to respond to news by pretending to have known all along is as old as the hills and has nothing to do with you.

For a lot of people, especially if you were raised in a conservative environment, coming out is the process of admitting to earlier dishonesty—admitting you were dishonest with your friends in high school, possibly even admitting you were dishonest with yourself. Many people are taught in sex-ed that same-sex attraction is a phase that will pass, and they assume they're still just in that phase and it hasn't passed yet, and for them coming out is the self-realization that it isn't a phase and isn't going to pass. Other people are legitimately attracted to people of both sexes, and coming out means admitting to being bisexual.

Here's what you don't realize: No one worth your time actually gives a flying fuck. It seems like they do, but they don't. They don't care if you're gay, they don't care if you're bisexual, they don't care if you're straight. They care if you're being dishonest with yourself and the people around you. Telling the truth will make you feel so much better, and you'll gain surprising insight into who your real friends and family are. There is no way of knowing how people will respond. But the good people, the morally superior people, the ones whose opinion you should care about—they're gonna be fine with it.

Where to Go to College If You're Gay

You're going to want to avoid Brigham Young University, that university that Jerry Falwell started, and anything with "Christ" in the name. You're going to want to avoid the South and a lot of the Midwest. You'll be fine in Chicago, Illinois, or Madison, Wisconsin, but in general you want to head for the coasts. Whatever you do, avoid those schools with beautiful architecture and nothing but fields for hundreds of miles; if you're already at one of those schools and the atmosphere is ridiculous and suffocating, transfer somewhere better as soon as possible. The bigger the city, the happier you'll be. You need to be introduced to the full spectrum of what the world has to offer, and you need to be around other gay people so that you can figure out this side of yourself and so that you can find someone to kiss.

The History of Gay People in a Few Paragraphs

....

There have been gays as long as there have been people. There have also been gay bees as long as there have been bees, gay penguins as long as there have been penguins, gay dolphins, gay seagulls, gay killer whales, gay bison, gay raccoons, gay elephants, gay moths, gay lions, gay caribou, gay turtles, gay cheetahs, gay lizards, gay fruit flies (rim shot!), gay dogs, and gay cats. A disproportionate number of People Who Changed the World are believed to have been gay. (Back before being gay was okay, the gays had lots of time on their hands for changing the world.) The guy who broke the Nazi code to lead the U.S. to victory in World War II was a homo, and so was the guy who came up with Keynesian economics, and so were Plato and Socrates and Sappho and Alexander the Great, to say nothing of Leonardo da Vinci and Michelangelo and Gertrude Stein and Eleanor Roosevelt and the Indigo Girls.

The gay civil rights movement started in 1969 in New York City, shortly after Judy Garland died, when a bunch of homos harassed by the cops at a gay bar called the Stonewall Inn decided they weren't going to take shit from the cops anymore. They chanted funny slogans and did chorus-line kicks. "I remember thinking this was going to be the first funny revolution," says Edmund White, who was there. Sometimes it wasn't that funny. The first openly gay politician elected to public office in the United States was San Francisco's Harvey Milk; he was shot and killed shortly thereafter.

Then came AIDS, a word Ronald Reagan refused to say or do anything about, leading to tens of thousands of deaths in the '80s and '90s, and nearly wiping out a generation. HIV, which causes AIDS, is still a serious disease, but with expensive treatment it can usually be managed. Still, not worth it. (Wear a condom, okay?) The discovery of treatments to keep people with HIV alive are largely thanks to activism in the lesbian community—the men were so busy dying that if it weren't for the women, gay acceptance and gay health wouldn't be where it is today.

Politically, liberals/progressives/Democrats are generally friendly to gay people and gay equality; Republicans, not so much (see also How to Know If You're a Republican or a Democrat, page 177.) Some Republicans with mainstream support continue to describe gays and lesbians as fundamentally immoral. Feel free to mercilessly hate these people for their fundamentally un-American stance on your rights. The Constitution clearly says that everyone shall be treated equally.

On Gay People Sleeping With Straight People

Actually falling in love (or even strongly in like) with, say, a straight person if you're a gay one is stupid, but sleeping with them is awesome—you get to see them adorably nervous, you get to be part of a big secret, you get to brag to your gay friends that you slept with a straight one. But again, it's stupid and you shouldn't

make a practice of it. If the stars align and you somehow get the right straight person drunk on the right night, you might feel like you're conquering that which you were most frightened of in high school (the straight person), but the truth is you're just setting yourself up to be conquered by them in a whole new way—defeated by their inevitable disinterest. Sexuality being a spectrum, almost every person is a little bit interested in those of their same sex, but making too much of that, assuming a little experimentation is more than just a little experimentation, puts you in the path of embarrassment and rejection. Sleeping with a straight person can be flattering, leading you to think you're special, that the rules don't apply to you, but rules always have their way in the end: Straight people want to be with straight people. Bisexual people who seem straight usually want to continue to seem straight.

How to Have Sex With a Man If You're a Man

A man puts his penis in another man and gay sex is born. But seriously: Unlike the exaggerated depictions would have you believe, many gay people never have anal sex, preferring instead to stick to making out, stroking each other's dicks, and oral sex. You should do likewise at first with any new partner you have. Making out with someone while stroking each other's dicks is safe and intimate and fun. Some STIs can be transmitted simply through contact, so you want to make sure you know and trust someone

before you go there. Once you feel like you can trust someone, you've asked about their sexual history, and you've asked if they have any STIs (if anything looks iffy, don't go there), you can graduate to doing more.

HOW TO HAVE ORAL SEX

What feels good to a man varies from man to man, but the general idea is to put your hand around the dick, cover the head with your mouth, and move your hand and mouth up and down together. Tell him to let you know before he comes or you might get a mouthful. If you want a mouthful, tell him that, too, but keep in mind that HIV is transmitted through semen, so if you have any cuts or canker sores, you're putting yourself at risk (if a low risk).

HOW TO HAVE ANAL SEX

When you're ready for anal sex—never have anal sex on a first date—you're going to need a condom, a lot of lube, and a lot of time. You don't want to rush it. Terminology lesson: The guy doing the fucking is the "top," and the guy getting fucked is the "bottom," no matter what position you do it in. The top will need to use his fingers to get the bottom excited and warmed up. One finger at first, then two fingers . . . then check in with the bottom and see if he's ready for your dick. Then roll on a condom, cover it in lube, cover the hole in still more lube, and go slowly. The bottom will be in pain until his muscles learn to relax and accept the sensation. It will take time. And still more lube.

How to Have Sex With a Woman If You're a Woman

Masturbate. A lot. Try different positions, different toys, different orifices (and beyond). Try for different types of orgasms—don't just go for a direct hit (unless you only have five minutes in a public bathroom). Indulge yourself; foreplay isn't just for when other people are around. Play with your fantasies, kinks, and desires. Read up on female sexuality and erotica. Confidence is key when it comes to sex—and the more you try out, the more you will know what works for you, and the less timid you'll be about your own and other people's bodies. Plus, that post-orgasm glow looks really good on you.

Communicate. A lot. Everyone's bodies (and brains) are different, even when you are working with similar parts. Rid yourself of preconceived notions about what ladies do with lady-parts. You don't have to be romantic and slow. Don't be afraid to fuck. Ask for and take what you want (remembering to make sure everyone involved is on board, of course). Embrace the fluidity that female sexuality has to offer, and play with all the tools you were given and the ones you've bought.

Your hands are your primary tools, so get ready to get arm-deep. Keep your nails trimmed, get latex/latex-free gloves, and lube. With patience and lots of talking, you can look forward to fisting, G-spot orgasms, and ejaculating. Strap-ons can also be powerful and exciting. Psychic dick is an amazing thing to experience—so if you

are game, it's worth investing in. (Any previously acquired cock-sucking skills can still come in handy when working with silicone.) And don't neglect your classic oral-sex techniques.

5. HOW TO SLEEP WITH YOUR PROFESSOR

BY PROFESSOR X

arly in my teaching career, I found a note slipped under my office door: "You're the sexiest professor on campus and if you can figure out who I am then you can have me." The note was more confusing than thrilling, especially since it was from a woman and I'm gay. Actually, I was a little threatened by the note—even as a misidentified object of desire. Universities have gotten more puritan and corporate in the past 20 years, and I had just watched a dean get dragged through the spectacle of publicly defending himself against charges of mishandling sexual harassment complaints. He was finally forced to resign.

I pondered the note for a day before I took it to the chair of the

department. He quickly read it, then with a slow grin reached into a desk drawer and pulled out one of those clunky metal stamping machines that records the date and stamped the note "Received." He knew I was gay, and his crazy, Kafkaesque gesture was a good joke that made me relax.

Universities have changed a lot, but there are still premodern aspects, like the classroom autonomy professors often enjoy and sometimes abuse. Deans can say what they want and have certain weapons in their arsenal, but a tenured professor usually has a remarkable degree of freedom in the classroom. The best professors care about what they are teaching and do give a damn whether or not students learn. The best teachers have an unschooled and unteachable talent to persuade and lead students toward one truth or another. Teaching is a form of seduction. At the same time, universities and colleges just happen to be hotbeds of sexual exploration and discovery for young men and women recently released from parental supervision. Bedding a professor is high on the student trophy list. Students are young, smooth, lean, and sometimes available—a high temptation for some colleagues. It can get messy.

Crazy rumors circulated for years, with sorority girls claiming to have slept with me or definitively knowing a girl who had. When I started getting unsolicited invitations and anonymous notes from young men, I was less amused. If colleagues heard that I was rumored to be fooling around with a young woman, they wouldn't take it seriously, but an athletic, handsome, creative, and sexy man—that's another story. I remember discussing one particularly

persistent brilliant and sexy male student with a doctor friend, who told me that physicians often negotiate a similar blurred zone of attraction, authority, and ethics. He had one simple principle: "Never, never, never sleep with anyone crazier than you."

The student in question wasn't clinically crazy, but he was in one of those frenzies that Alcibiades describes in Plato's *Symposium*. He was brilliant, in love with somebody he thought was smarter than he was, and eager to get into bed with him. He was a little crazed. It would have been easy for me to sleep with him, but probably stupid: He was unpredictable and dramatic. Over the course of a semester, I negotiated my escape from his advances. He finally graduated and moved to Manhattan, where he became a painter and gay activist. (I ran into him one day near the New York Public Library; we had a nice exchange, and he encouraged me to "get back in touch.")

Students like to flirt with professors, especially during office hours. It's harmless, insincere, and flattering to those of us who have annual physicals. But when students want attention, I often turn a blind eye. I have a reputation for being a misanthrope when it comes to student social events and sit with a quasi scowl until I excuse myself from the proceedings. I met my last serious challenge at a department dinner for majors, and even though he was interested in me, I was clueless. He signed up for a seminar I was teaching, and other professors who knew that the student was gay asked what I thought of him. They were all pretty convinced he was the smartest student in the department, and he was awkwardly

gay in the most adorable way. I started to warm up, pay attention, and feel some sympathy for him. We began an unspoken ritual where he would show up at my office before class and ask me if I wanted a cup of coffee. We would then walk to the café together, chat about nothing, and then walk to class together. I could tell he was nervous, and I thought that made him even more adorable. We slowly graduated to the occasional lunch, and I thought our conversations were more like mentoring sessions—the sympathetic gay professor coaching the young student in queer matters.

Then one day he sprung it on me: He couldn't go with me and a group of students on an overnight trip because it would just be too difficult; his interests in me were not just academic. I was impressed with how direct and honest he was, and I told him I understood but that nothing could happen between us, and I wasn't interested in him anyway because he was too young and I didn't want to settle down. He took it well, but I sensed it was tough on him. About a month later, he invited me to lunch and asked if I was sure I wasn't interested in having a relationship. It was painful, and my advice to him at the time was to hang out with more gay people; I told him (thinking back to my own experience in the '80s) to experiment and shop around, have more experience before he thought about settling into a relationship.

Nice advice, especially for the 1980s, but graduation came, he became legal, and I was surprised, truly, to realize that one needs to be careful about these things. *Love* was happening. It is still happening several years later. There is an age difference, to be

sure, but no power or authority issues. He seduced me, but now we're partners.

Teachers and students have been falling in love forever. If you're just looking to bed your professor, you might have a good shot, but remember that it could easily get messy and it might also be terrifying for him—unless you want to ruin his career, you need to take your diploma before you take off your clothes. If you're a professor, remember how awkward it will feel when you walk across campus and see that guy (now clothed) with his schoolmates, talking and turning their heads to look at you. A student might be easy and tempting, but he could also develop a very painful crush on you, and you need to be responsible for the collateral damage. The bottom line is this: Think, respect each other, don't use stupid clichéd excuses, and don't fuck anyone crazier than you. Oh, and if you're in graduate school, all bets are off.

Professor X is an actual professor.

6. SAVAGE LOVE, COLLEGE EDITION

A Collection of **DAN SAVAGE**'s Best Advice About Drunkenly Hitting on Roommates, Having Forced Sex with an Ex in a Parking Lot, the Right Way to Explore Polyamory, the Wrong Way to Deal with Annoying Parents, and More

So I Have This Roommate

. . . .

A FEW NIGHTS AGO, *I got drunk and knocked on my roommate's door and confessed my attraction to him while he was lying in bed in nothing more than his skivvies. And then I asked him if I could sleep in his room because our other roommate—whose bedroom is*

directly above mine—was having sex so loudly that I couldn't sleep. Which was true, but it clearly didn't make the bed of the roommate I was drunkenly confessing to the appropriate alternative. Not being able to sleep on work nights is sometimes a real problem, but one to be addressed with her, not used as drunken fodder to get into someone else's bed.

I feel pathetic and embarrassed for having thrown myself at my roommate and completely freaked out that I got wasted enough to do something I have daydreamed about but wouldn't do sober. But much more importantly, I think my behavior did not reflect active consent, trashed my roommate's boundaries, and was generally creepy—all characteristics of sexual assaulters.

I am biologically female, and if the situation were reversed, I would commit a huge double standard because I would back any woman who did not feel safe continuing to live with a dude who did what I did. I feel like I should be held accountable and move out immediately, though my housemate has told me he doesn't feel threatened and that I should stay.

Help. I feel like a total piece of shit for having done this and can't stop wondering . . .

Am I A Sexual Predator?

Calm the fuck down—and no more women's studies classes for you, okay? I think you've had quite enough, and I'm cutting you off.

Look, AIASP, you didn't assault anyone, you're not a predator, you shouldn't have to move out. You made a drunken,

ill-advised-in-retrospect pass at a roommate. If that makes someone a "sexual predator," AIASP, then we'd better build walls around our better universities and start calling 'em all penitentiaries.

As for that double standard: In light of your recent experience—you made a drunken pass at someone who wasn't interested in you—you might want to revisit the assumptions you've made about men who make passes, drunken and otherwise, at women who aren't interested in them. Making a pass is not grounds for eviction or conviction. It's how a person makes a pass (did you pounce or did you ask?) and how a person reacts if the pass is rebuffed (did you graciously take no for an answer or were you a complete asshole about it?) that matters.

Of course, men's passes at women—roommates and otherwise—exist in a context of male sexual violence. So it's understandable that a woman might feel uncomfortable living with a dude who did what you did. But if the dude wasn't a creep about it and graciously took no for an answer (if the answer was no), perhaps he should be judged as an individual and not as someone who bears responsibility for the collective crimes committed by members of his sex throughout history.

And even if you were an asshole about that no, AIASP, that still wouldn't make you a sexual predator. You're only a sexual predator—or guilty of sexual assault—if you refuse to take no for an answer and force yourself on someone. (Or if you go after someone who is incapable of granting consent.) You didn't force yourself on anyone. All you're guilty of, AIASP, is asking someone whom you

wanted to fuck if he wanted to fuck you. It's a legit question, and no one gets fucked without asking it.

And that simple question doesn't magically become sexual assault or harassment when the answer is no.

I'M HERPES-FREE, *but I found out today that my roommate has contracted it. He has a sore but won't see a doctor about it because he says he's embarrassed. We share the same bathroom, so I knew I would have to be diligent about that. But now I am freaking out: Not long after he shared this information, my 7-month-old puppy runs into his room and proceeds to cover my roommate's face in kisses. I've called the vet and my medical provider, and while they both agree that my pup cannot contract the STD, they cannot rule out the pup passing the infection on to me. Please advise. I would like to know how to best handle this situation.*

Scared To Death

Wouldn't it be great if being paranoid about contracting herpes was the only way to contract herpes?

Look, STD, lots of people self-diagnose themselves with herpes when all they have is an innocuous little cut or sore near their mouth or genitals. People who are too embarrassed/ridiculous to go see their doctors are highly likely to arrive at a herpes misdiagnosis. So calm the fuck down.

Even if your roommate does have herpes, STD, you're not going to get it from sharing a toilet—unless you and the roommate have

invented a novel new way of taking a dump. And you're not going to get it from your damn dog. For his own sake, your roommate shouldn't allow your dog to lick his open sores (who does he think he is? Lazarus?), herpes-related or not, and if you're really freaking out about your promiscuously affectionate new dog, well, you can make up your mind to refrain from kissing any animal that drinks out of toilets, licks its own ass, and laps up vomit.

MY ROOMMATE IS ASTOUNDINGLY HOT. *Her room is being repaired (the ceiling fell in), and, at her request, I'm letting her and her boyfriend sleep in my room while I take the couch. I've been able to contain my attraction just fine up to now, but the minute she entered my space I had this feeling that all bets are off. I'm considering spying on her with a hidden surveillance cam. If I had video of this girl naked, let alone being fucked, I could happily beat off to the footage for the rest of my life. Obviously it's a breach of trust, and I'm a shitty roommate for considering it. I have a few concerns. Is this normal? Assuming that there's no way she could find out and that I kept the video to myself and myself only, would it be so wrong? What is her reasonable expectation of privacy once she enters my room?*

Thanks In Advance

While it's normal to contemplate, even obsess about, something you know is wrong, secretly videotaping your roommate, even if she's "in your space," isn't just an asshole move. It's an illegal move

in most places, and the consequences for asshole moves involving digital images can be dire. And until submitting to videotaping is widely understood to be a known risk of sleeping in someone else's bedroom, your roommate and her boyfriend have an entirely reasonable expectation of privacy.

As for no-way-she-could-ever-find-out, I could sneak into your house and use your toothbrush as a sound, and you'd never find out. And although it would hurt me more than it would hurt you, TIA, it would still be wrong—even if there was no way short of DNA testing that you would ever find out. And while you may intend to keep the video to yourself—such the gentleman—what if your laptop gets stolen? What if you take your computer in for repairs and someone makes a copy? Digital images—photos, video, whatever—are too easy to lose control over.

Don't do it, TIA.

MY TWO ROOMMATES *are in the same frat. Roommate A is a great guy, but maybe a bit too nice: Recently, his GF cheated on him and he forgave her. Her infidelity did not come as a surprise to the rest of us. When she's drunk, she acts inappropriately. She gets touchy and says suggestive things—it's way beyond friendly flirting.*

Anyway, Roommate B came into my room the other night and confessed that, a week or so before Roommate A's GF cheated on him, she propositioned another member of his fraternity—let's call him OG (Other Guy)—while Roommate A was away. OG refused,

to his credit, and relayed the story to Roommate B, but swore him to secrecy.

Is it my place to tell Roommate A about his GF's behavior? I don't know OG well enough to tell him to tell Roommate A, and Roommate B won't tell Roommate A. Everyone agrees that it's a fucked-up situation. I mean, no one really knows how many times GF has fucked around on my roommate. What's your take?

Friend Really Over Strumpet's Treachery

All you've got, FROST, is hearsay—what Roommate B told you about what OG told him about Roommate A's GF—and hearsay isn't admissible in court. But this isn't a trial, it's a friendship, and sometimes friendship requires us to pass along hearsay and/or highly credible gossip.

What's that lovely saying that sometimes drops from the oh-so-fuckable mouths of frat boys? Oh, yes: *Bros before hos.* Usually I find that phrase offensive and misogynistic, FROST, but in this instance it applies.

Tell Roommate A what you know. If his GF is making passes at everything on campus with a cock, Roommate A has a right to know for his own health and safety. His GF also needs to learn a valuable lesson: She's got to set up her cheatin' game—fuck people outside of her boyfriend's social circle, for starters—if she intends to cheat on all the men she's with over the course of her life. Getting her ass dumped for sloppy technique in college will help her get her cheating act together by the time she marries some poor bastard.

And finally, FROST, there's a chance—an outside one—that Roommate A already knows and doesn't care, either because he and GF have an open relationship or he's turned on by his girlfriend "cheating" on him. If Roommate A doesn't dump his GF after you break the news, FROST, you're not obligated to inform him about any other trouble his GF gets into. Rest assured, she's telling him all about it while he fucks her senseless.

So I Have This Religion

I HEARD AN INTERVIEW *with you about your It Gets Better campaign. I was saddened and frustrated with your comments regarding people of faith and their perpetuation of bullying. As someone who loves the Lord and does not support gay marriage, I can honestly say I was heartbroken to hear about the young man who took his own life.*

If your message is that we should not judge people based on their sexual preference, how do you justify judging entire groups of people for any other reason (including their faith)? There is no part of me that took any pleasure in what happened to that young man.

To that end, to imply that I would somehow encourage my children to mock, hurt, or intimidate another person for any reason is completely unfounded and offensive. Being a follower of Christ is, above all things, a recognition that we are all imperfect, fallible, and in desperate need of a savior. We cannot believe that we are better or more worthy than other people.

Please consider your viewpoint, and please be more careful with your words in the future.

L.R.

I'm sorry your feelings were hurt by my comments.

No, wait. I'm not. Gay kids are *dying*. So let's try to keep things in perspective: Fuck your feelings.

A question: Do you "support" atheist marriage? Interfaith marriage? Divorce and remarriage? All are legal, all go against Christian and/or traditional ideas about marriage, and yet there's no "Christian" movement to deny marriage rights to atheists or people marrying outside their respective faiths or people divorcing and remarrying. Why the hell not?

Sorry, L.R., but so long as you support the denial of marriage rights to same-sex couples, it's clear that you do believe that some people—straight people—are "better or more worthy" than others.

And sorry but you are partly responsible for the bullying and physical violence being visited on vulnerable LGBT children. The kids of people who see gay people as sinful or damaged or disordered and unworthy of full civil equality—even if those people strive to express their bigotry in the politest possible way (at least when they happen to be addressing a gay person)—learn to see gay people as sinful, damaged, disordered, and unworthy. And while there may not be any gay adults or couples where you live, or at your church, or in your workplace, I promise you that there are

gay and lesbian children in your schools. And while you can attack gays and lesbians only at the ballot box, nice and impersonally, your children have the option of attacking actual gays and lesbians, in person, in real time.

Real gay and lesbian children. Not political abstractions, not "sinners." Gay and lesbian children.

Try to keep up: The dehumanizing bigotries that fall from the lips of "faithful Christians," and the lies about us that vomit out from the pulpits of churches that "faithful Christians" drag their kids to on Sundays, give your children license to verbally abuse, humiliate, and condemn the gay children they encounter at school. And many of your children—having listened to Mom and Dad talk about how gay marriage is a threat to family and how gay sex makes their magic sky friend Jesus cry—feel justified in physically abusing the LGBT children they encounter in their schools. You don't have to explicitly "encourage [your] children to mock, hurt, or intimidate" queer kids. Your encouragement—along with your hatred and fear—is implicit. It's here, it's clear, and we're seeing the fruits of it: dead children.

Oh, and those same dehumanizing bigotries that fill your straight children with hate? They fill your gay children with suicidal despair. And you have the nerve to ask me to be more careful with my words?

Did that hurt to hear? Good. But it couldn't have hurt nearly as much as what was said and done to Asher Brown and Justin Aaberg and Billy Lucas and Cody Barker and Seth Walsh—day in, day out for years—at schools filled with bigoted little monsters created not

in the image of a loving God, but in the image of the hateful and false "followers of Christ" they call Mom and Dad.

I'M A STRAIGHT MALE COLLEGE STUDENT *in a relationship, which had been going great. The only incongruity was that, for a religious reason, I don't want to have penetrative vaginal sex before marriage. I'm up for anything else—I would eat her out, piss on her, whatever else—but not vaginal sex. I made this clear at the beginning. My girlfriend started bringing up how she wanted to have "actual" sex. I told her, "I love you, and if you need to fuck other guys, go for it." To my relief, she was offended by the suggestion.*

A week later, she confessed that she had slept with someone. I feel like I can't trust her now, and I can't bring myself to sleep in her bed anymore. I feel like a hypocrite, since I brought up the idea of her sleeping with someone else in the first place. But I was unprepared for the reality, since she berated me for making the proposal at all. Still, I told her to do this. She regrets the hookup. I don't know if I'm even asking for advice. I just wonder if I'm acting childishly.

Wishing Ancillary Fucking Felt Less Emotionally Ruinous

Your dilemma is interesting, WAFFLER, but you know what I'm more interested in? I'd really be interested in finding out which particular faith tradition frowns on penetrative vaginal intercourse before marriage but smiles on eating pussy and piss scenes and

okays women having vaginal intercourse before marriage so long as they're having it with guys they don't intend to marry. That sounds like a church I'd like to visit. Hell, that sounds like a church I should be tithing to.

Look, WAFFLER, doing everything-but-sticking-your-dick-in for religious reasons is deeply silly. If you're going to be in a sexual relationship, be in a sexual relationship. I promise you that any God who frowns on fucking-pussy-before-marriage also frowns on piss-play-before-marriage and eating-pussy-before-marriage.

As for your dilemma, WAFFLER, either you need to find a girlfriend who wants what you want—or doesn't want what you don't want—or you need to stop playing bullshit games and start fucking the girl you've got.

YOU WERE RECOMMENDED TO ME *by an acquaintance familiar with your column and podcast. I am a 20-year-old male, and as such have certain desires that almost all 20-year-old males have (desires of a sexual nature). However, I am deeply religious. Religion has been for me a source of strength in my times of weakness, a rock in the times of storm, and above all a home to return to when I have lost my path. In the teachings of my particular religion, to indulge the particular desires I am experiencing will condemn me to fates too grotesque to mention. I am rational enough to realize that there is no way that I can "pray away" these desires. My question is this: How does one prepare for a life of celibacy and solitude (as that is what is required of*

me to remain a member of this particular faith)? Based on what my friend has told me, I know you have little respect for religious practices and beliefs. However, these desires are not exactly something I can talk about with other members of my spiritual community. And while I am currently seeking counseling related to other issues, I was wondering what a so-called expert on sex and sexuality would have to say.

Clever Acronyms Escape Me

Get over yourself, faggot.

If it's possible for you to act on your unnamed-but-easily-identified desires in an ethical manner—if you desire to do whatever it is you desire to do with consenting adults who desire to take their turn doing it to you—this so-called expert on sexuality thinks you should crawl down off that cross and find yourself a boyfriend already. ("Pray away" the gay? I'm guessing you're Christian, probably Catholic.) And if you experience a moment's anxiety the first time you stick your ass in the air—pull the Jesus stick out first!—just remind yourself that things have been crawling on top of each other and madly humping away for 850 million years. Sex came first, then humanity (200,000ish years ago), then religion came along tens of thousands of years after that. Which may explain why religion, when pitted against sex (really old) and human nature (pretty old), always loses. Always.

If you're on the cross, CAEM, it's because you put yourself up there. Which means you're not some poor mortal trapped between

a cosmic rock and an existential hard place; you're just another closeted cocksucker with a martyr complex.

Look, kiddo, you get one life, one chance at happiness. If it gives you a spiritual semi to fantasize about a God who created you gay but forbids you to act on your emotional and sexual attraction to men, knock your damn self out. But you can have a boyfriend and Jesus, too—look at the pope—you just have to do what people have been doing since the first terrified idiot invented the first bullshit religion: improvise. Find yourself a brand-new religion or sect, or jettison the bits of your current faith that don't work for you. If you know anything about the history of Christianity—and it sounds like you don't—then you know that the revisions began before the body was cold. No reason to stop now.

And finally, CAEM, there is no God—you do realize that, right? No hell below us, above us only sky, etc.

So I Just Discovered Anal Sex

MY BOYFRIEND AND I *are straight college students, and he's always wanting to try new things. Recently, he asked to put a finger in my ass while we were having sex. Someone did that to me before, but it felt uncomfortable and it kinda hurt. I told my boyfriend that he could do it once and then I would decide whether to let it continue. So we tried it. It still felt uncomfortable and still kinda hurt. But I never came so hard in my life!*

Now the question: If it's uncomfortable, but it made me feel amazing and come really hard, what should I do? Continue with it?

Or tell him to find some other way of getting me to that point again?

Presently Obsessing Over Totally Extreme Reaction

You could ask the boyfriend to stick a finger in one of your armpits—or in an eye, a nostril, your toaster—but unless your pit/eye/nostril/toaster is wired the way your butt appears to be, POOTER, no amount of pit/eye/nostril/toaster fingering is gonna jack up your orgasms quite the way that finger in your butt did.

So here's what you're gonna do, POOTER: You're gonna breathe deep, you're gonna take things slow, you're gonna use more lube, and you're gonna spend more time warming up the outside of your butt before anything goes in. (Tell the boyfriend he can finger your butt for 10 minutes after he rims it for 20.) Do it right, POOTER, and pretty soon you won't be able to look at those 10 fingers of his without thinking about the kick ass, anal-enhanced orgasms you'll be having when you can only see nine.

I AM AN 18-YEAR-OLD FEMALE COLLEGE FRESHMAN. *My boy friend is also 18. He recently confided in me that he wanted to wear my panties while I wore his boxers and fucked him in the ass with a dildo. I have been reading your column since I was 13. Had I never read your column, I might have assumed my boyfriend was gay or thought he was gross or thought I was gross for liking the idea. Instead, I picked out some panties that looked sweet on him, and we had a wonderful time. Thank you so much!*

Loves Boys In Panties

No, thank *you*, LBIP, because every time a straight girl sticks something up a straight boy's ass, a bigoted state representative dies a little inside.

I AM A COMPLETELY STRAIGHT GUY. *I am madly in love with my girlfriend. One night, she was giving me oral and stuck a finger in my ass. I was uncomfortable at first, but in a little time I began to like it. I found it felt so good. Now my girlfriend asked if I wanted to try a butt plug. At first I said, "Yes!" But now, the more I think about it, I am starting to think it may be gay. My question: Is there something gay about using a butt plug?*

Guy With Anal Interests

I've dedicated my life to reassuring panicky straight boys that a little anal stimulation won't make 'em gay. My oft-stated position: If a guy and a girl are doing it during sex—whatever it is, whatever it looks like—it's straight sex. And, yes, that includes a pair of straight girls making out to turn on a straight boy, as well as the far less common straight-boys-making-out-to-turn-on-a-straight-girl scenario.

But no more. From now on, I intend to sow gay panic when and where I can. Maybe straight men, who vote in overwhelming numbers for the various antigay shit on their ballots, won't be so quick to strip gay people of their civil rights if they're worried that one false move—or one finger up the butt—can turn them gay. So for the record, breeder boys: A finger in the butt can make you gay, using a butt plug can make you gay, doing it doggy style can

make you gay, playing with your nipples can make you gay, fucking a woman in the ass can make you gay, wiping from front to back can make you gay, standing up to pee can make you gay, and watching dudes hump dudes on ESPN—Ultimate Fighting Championship— for sure makes you gay.

So I've Been Thinking About Polyamory

I'M A BISEXUAL WOMAN, *age 20, and I am threesome-ing it with my best friend and her boyfriend during a stay abroad. I knew the girl (mostly straight) beforehand. She thinks it's hot when I participate—i.e., when it's three of us in bed—but she gets jealous when her boyfriend and I do anything without her. I don't get jealous when she is alone with her boyfriend, and he doesn't yet get jealous when she and I do things alone.*

She doesn't want to be possessive, but she's got alarms going off. Which is odd because in two months I'll be gone and they'll both be staying in Europe. It feels like she's suddenly setting a lot of limits. We have a blast when we're all together, but we have no real ground rules. I want this to work!

Bi Girl Interrupted

Gee, BGI, I'm shocked things aren't going well—I mean, you have "no real ground rules," and as everyone knows, neglecting to establish ground rules is the secret to threesome-ing success.

Wait, did I say the secret to threesome-ing success? I'm sorry, BGI, I meant failure. To ensure the failure of a threesome—whether you're threesome-ing your way through an evening or a summer abroad—it's crucial that you refrain from establishing ground rules. Don't talk about your expectations, just make assumptions; don't make sure everyone's on the same page, just stomp around the minefield of love and lust until the whole fucking thing blows up in your faces.

I trust you're detecting sarcasm, BGI.

Here's what I suspect the problem is: You're operating under the assumption that you're an equal partner in this threesome, BGI, and that this is a sort of quasi-poly arrangement you're enjoying with your best friend and her boyfriend. Share and share alike, right? But your best friend views you as a side attraction. She sees you as something—pardon me, *someone*—that she and the boyfriend brought into *their* relationship, not someone who they've brought into the *relationship* itself.

In other words: They're the couple—they were a couple before you came along, and they're planning to be a couple after you're gone. If you're unclear on that concept, BGI, it's because the three of you failed to establish clear ground rules and expectations and now you're confused, she's jealous, and he's either taking advantage or feeling caught in the middle.

Luckily it's not too late for the three of you to sit down and establish some ground rules. It may be that your friend, while comfortable with the idea of you and her messing around without

the boyfriend, isn't comfortable with the idea of you and the boyfriend messing around without her. You may regard that limitation as unfair and irrational; the boyfriend may regard it as unfair and irrational; I may regard it as unfair and irrational. But if you want this to work, BGI, then you'll make allowances for your best friend's comfort levels and security and honor her limitations.

And if you don't wanna honor 'em, you're free to go.

I'M A STRAIGHT COLLEGE GUY, *age 21, and I share a house with some buddies and a couple. This couple has been together for four years. They're both quite sexual, but she's got more libido than he does. I've got a big sex drive, too. Both of them have stated an openness to polyamorous situations. She started flirting with me, and flirting turned into no-sex threesomes with her and her BF every few nights.*

I'm perfectly fine with poly, or I wouldn't be doing this, but it feels a bit awkward fingering her or sucking on her nipples while her boyfriend is in the room, or even the same bed. Both of us guys are straight and have no desire to see the other naked, so there's none of that going on. I've got no beef with guys who like beef, but being in a sexual situation with another guy—like the one going on here—makes me uncomfortable. And anyway, I feel like he's the "primary" one, the one she loves and kisses, so I move over whenever he shows interest. This is reinforced because she said that she didn't feel comfortable kissing other guys—although fingering is fine (?)—and I get the impression that he's not entirely

happy that I'm cuddling and/or fingering his girlfriend while he plays Dawn of War five feet away from their bed.

I'm fine with being the "secondary" guy. But I'd much rather have some privacy if we—meaning me and her—are gonna try to get each other off, particularly if this arrangement of ours should progress to actual sex. But this is tough, since there's nowhere else in the house to go other than their room. Incidentally, we haven't told our other friends/housemates about this, although they could probably put two and two together; she screams in orgasm, and half an hour later I say good night and go back down to my room.

Any advice for making the situation more comfortable for all involved?

Can't Think Of A Clever Name

You're fingering her, you're sucking her tits, you're getting her off (screaming orgasms induced dicklessly), she's getting you off (your orgasms induced somehow or other)—which means, CTOACN, that this can't be described as a "no-sex" arrangement. You're not having vaginal intercourse, you're not kissing the girl, but you're having sex, and a lot of it.

But I wouldn't slap a 10-dollar word like "polyamorous" on what you're doing. You may be in a polyamorous relationship someday—with this couple, with some other couple—but all you're really doing at the moment is "messing around."

Okay, CTOACN, it sounds like this girl is pretty up front about what she's comfortable doing—no kissing, no vaginal intercourse

(for you)—and clear about her boundaries. You need to be similarly assertive. Tell them both that you're not comfortable messing around while he's in the room. So instead of playing Dawn of War while you two mess around, her boyfriend could head to the library, go for a walk, do some reading in the communal space of your shared house, or—hey—go play Dawn of War in your room for a while.

If he balks, CTOACN, then you may want to reconsider the assumptions you've made about him. You're not comfortable with any hint of guy-on-guy, but he may want to be in the room while you're messing around with his girlfriend because he digs that hint. I'm not saying that he's bi, or that he wants to get with you, as the kids were only too recently saying—but I'm not saying he isn't bi or doesn't want to get with you, either. I guess what I'm saying is . . .

Considering (1) his presence every time you're messing around with her (surely the library, the living room, or your room would've occurred to him if he were uncomfortable being in the same room while you fingered his girlfriend), (2) the limitations she's placed on the kind of sex she'll have with you, and (3) his tendency to suddenly "show interest" after you've been messing around with his girlfriend (at which point you "move over" and, presumably, out), I'm thinking this girl's boyfriend is into cuckolding-lite.

Not that there's anything wrong with that, of course. But it could mean asking for quality time alone with his girlfriend would bring the messing around to an end.

I'M A 21-YEAR-OLD WOMAN *with bi-curious tendencies who's been in a committed relationship for four years. He's sweet and*

kind. We share a lot of interests and get along very well. Thing is, I don't know if I'm meant to be in a committed relationship. For the past year and a half, I've been thinking about what things would be like with another man. I also frequently imagine what it might be like to sleep with another girl. In fact, whenever I'm masturbating, I get more excited by lesbian scenarios than straight scenarios—although I've never been able to come. I've never experienced an orgasm. But that's another can of worms.

I'm open to the possibility of a threesome, but my boyfriend isn't. He's completely against the idea. From the start, I've never hidden the fact that I've never reached orgasm, and he's never created any macho drama about that.

I've slowly come to the realization that I'm no longer sexually attracted to my boyfriend. I don't have the motivation to improve our sex life anymore. I just go through the motions. At the same time, my boyfriend remains my best friend, and I'm not willing to give up my best friend over sex. I want to keep him in my life, as he is my most important source of emotional support.

Have My Cake

You can have your current boyfriend, HMC, at the price of a lousy and uninspired sex life with a guy who doesn't give a shit about your pleasure—excuse me, a partner who hasn't created a lot of "macho drama" about the fact that you've never had an orgasm and isn't interested in helping you realize your fantasies—or you can find a new boyfriend and/or girlfriend and perhaps discover that

orgasms are easier to come by when you're with someone who (1) turns you on, and (2) gives a shit about your pleasure, and (3) hasn't come to symbolize the death of sexual possibility.

Giving up the current boyfriend means you'll have to find a new emotional tampon—excuse me, a new "source of emotional support"—but that's a price that you should be willing to pay, HMC, particularly at your age.

And if you don't want to find yourself boyfriendless and best-friendless ever again, HMC, in the future keep those roles separate.

I AM A 21-YEAR-OLD MALE *in a loving and committed relationship. The sex is great; the evenings together are great. It's a perfectly happy relationship except for this one thing: I can't get enough change. I want to be having sex with someone else. One girl is never going to be enough to make me happy.*

I have asked her about the possibility of having a threesome. She said she would never go for that, not MMF or FFM, and she is utterly against it and always will be. But I NEED more. Sad fact. What do I do?

Coming Up More

Look, CUM, you're 21 and you're not ready to settle down—or settle for one person—not yet anyway, maybe not ever. However lovely this girl is, however pleasant your evenings together are, you're not sexually compatible. There would be fewer divorces and less heartbreak if people were encouraged to view sexual

incompatibility as the deal breaker it inevitably becomes over time.

Dump the nice girl, be single, fuck around, and keep your eyes peeled for a girl who wants what you want, change and all.

So I Have These Parents

I NEED YOUR HELP. *I have entered into a period of my life where I am devoting all my mental resources toward my academics— grad school—and am not interested in dating. Thus, I bought a Real Doll so that I may enjoy fantastic masturbation during this loveless period. Unfortunately, while my parents were visiting, my mom discovered it and she reacted very, very badly.*

You see, my dear mother is a feminist.

She is very upset by the doll and believes that it is an indication that I have lost all respect for women. I do not feel this is true. I view myself as a feminist, and I realize this society sexually objectifies women. But I also believe that I can masturbate with a rubber woman and have wild fantasies and then come back to reality and respect everyone—men, women, others. My mother, however, is extremely upset, and we haven't been able to have a civil conversation since. I am hoping you can possibly give me some perspective.

Dolled Up

My perspective: Your masturbatory routines—including your masturbatory aids/aides—are none of your mother's fucking business.

And if your mother wants to be shocked by something, DU, it ought to be that her son-the-grad-student had $5K to plunk down on a sex toy.

Your options at this stage are pretty limited. You can apologize to your mother and tell her what she wants to hear ("You're right, Mom, I'm making an appointment with a therapist and donating my Real Doll to sex-starved grad students in Africa . . . "). Or you can tell your mother to fuck off and butt out ("It's my dick, Mom, and I'll stick it in whatever I want. You remember that 'my body, my choice' stuff, right?").

That said, DU, your claim that you bought a Real Doll so you could "enjoy fantastic masturbation during this loveless period" doesn't quite pass the smell-of-day-old-spunk-moldering-in-the-lifeless-orifice-of-a-silicone-dummy test. Most guys manage to tough out their loveless periods with the help of the porn industry and their own right hands. And most guys who opt for insanely expensive, life-size, hard-to-hide sex dolls do have issues with women—most are plagued by feelings of inadequacy, not superiority—so you may want to entertain the possibility that your mother might be right.

But even if you do have issues with women—still an if—they're still none of your mother's fucking business.

I AM A 21-YEAR-OLD BISEXUAL FEMALE. *I've never really been close with my mum, and since I moved away from home three years ago it's gotten worse. I know that she loves me because I'm her daughter, but I don't think she likes the young adult I'm growing into. Yet she insists I visit her and stay at her house for weeks when I have time off from*

college so she can talk me out of liking anything she hates. When I'm with my friends, I'm quite witty and outgoing, particularly about sex. But when I stay with her, my personality becomes crippled and stunted by her authority. I seem to just end up not saying anything at all for fear of offending her. Last year I stupidly told her that I like watching porn; now it's something that she's always bringing up. For example, I got into a conversation with her about a recent breakup and asked her if all men were like my cheating ex. She told me that she thought his cheating was my fault—because I watch porn, she said, I must have been sending out subliminal messages that I approve of women being sexually exploited.

She raised me to be a feminist, but I can't bring myself to ask her if she would kick up this much of a fuss if I were a 21-year-old man who watched porn. I don't know what to do to make her happy, short of having some sort of porn-aversion therapy. I feel really conflicted: Away from my mother, I feel like a confident, empowered young woman; when I'm with her, I feel like this mute, angry, introverted little victim.

I know exactly what I'd do if this were a relationship, but how should I resolve a difficult mother/daughter relationship?

Can I Dump My Mother?

If hanging out with your mother makes you miserable, CIDMM, don't hang out with your fucking mother. You're a 21-year-old adult—not a young adult, not someone "growing into" adulthood, but an adult already—and you're in no way obligated to spend all of your free time under your mother's roof. Head off with your friends

over college breaks, travel, watch porn. Head home for the holidays if you must. And since your mother is inclined to use the details of your personal life that you share with her against you, don't tell her anything about your personal life.

ONE OF MY BEST FRIENDS AT COLLEGE IS GAY. *I'm a straight female with my own boyfriend. We're going to be sophomores in the fall, and I feel like this is about the age where coming out to one's parents is in order. However, my friend's parents are conservative. His older brother is also gay—and when he came out, his parents cut off all funding for college and excommunicated him from the family, so my friend is understandably terrified.*

When his parents come to visit, I tag along on "dates" with him to "meet the parents." It's a free meal, but it feels a little dirty to lie to his mom and dad about how "in love" we are. Moreover, my friend is coming to my house in California this summer. I had said I would love for him to come visit—as a friend. But his parents think he's going to be staying with his girlfriend, and they're thinking of tagging along so they can finally meet their future in-laws, i.e., MY PARENTS. I feel like this is getting way out of hand. How far should we take this act?

I Should Win An Oscar

When you feel bad about lying, ISWAO, remind yourself that you're doing a good deed—you're doing God's work—every time you pass yourself off as this boy's girlfriend. Yes, you're lying to his mean-spirited, emotionally abusive parents, two complete shits who

deserve so much worse than simply being misled. And he only lies to them because—for the time being—he must.

You should ask him to do three things to secure your continued cooperation in this deception. First, he has to make a solemn promise that he will come out to his parents the day after he graduates. Second, he has to reach out to his excommunicated brother and, if his brother can be trusted to keep his secret, he has to come out to his brother. Third, he has to break up with you at the end of the school year.

The course of true love never did run smooth, as someone or other once said, so a painfully messy June breakup with his college girlfriend—right before summer break!—not only makes your friend's Potemkin heterosexuality that much more credible, it also gets you off the hook for this ill-advised summer visit. Then when September rolls around, ISWAO, you two crazy kids get back together. Repeat as necessary, i.e., be "on again" when his parents are in town, be "off again" when your parents are in town, over summer breaks, holidays, etc.

And help him look around for his next girlfriend—perhaps a lesbian student with similarly batshit parents—because he can't expect you to be his beard for your entire college career.

So I Have This Kink

. . . .

I RECENTLY READ THE NOVEL A Melon for Ecstasy *for an English class, and an interesting debate came up. It's about a guy who is attracted to trees and goes around drilling holes into trees so*

that he can "seal the deal." Though he feminizes the trees, he cares nothing about actual human females. The debate centered on this question: Is this man heterosexual? Or is he really gay? Is he having vaginal sex with a woman or anal sex with a man?

RF

If the male protagonist in *A Melon for Ecstasy* is having sexual intercourse with lady-trees—"feminized" trees—then the male protagonist is a true-blue, red-blooded, lady-tree-fucking straight boy, RF.

But it doesn't surprise me that a room full of mostly straight college students would seek to cast doubt on this character's heterosexuality. "Heterosexual" for many young people is practically synonymous with "normal." Introduce college-age straight kids to a not-so-normal heterosexual character, and they'll spend the rest of the afternoon searching for evidence that the dude is gay. He can't be straight—he's not normal! This explains the ability of some in your class to look at lady-tree fucking and see, of all things, "anal sex with a man." Isn't santorum bad enough? Do we have to worry about splinters now too? (Queer-studies kids who read homosexuality into obviously straight fictional characters are, for the record, just as annoying.)

I'M A YOUNG HETEROFLEXIBLE GUY *who has been a "sugar baby" for a handful of wealthy older guys. I love it! I get money, I have fun being with them, and the guys seem to like having me around.*

The problem is that I just got with a new guy who is really great except for one thing: He is HIV positive. I like the fact that he told me, and I am open to being with him sexually even though I am HIV negative and want to stay that way.

He is VERY submissive—he wants to be used and abused sexually, physically, and mentally. My question is, what kinds of sex acts are okay to do with this guy? I read on one site that him rimming me is fine, and on another that him giving me a blowjob with a condom is safe, too. But I can't find a site that specifically explains which sex acts are safe and which ones aren't when one person is positive and one person is negative.

Help In Virginia

It's pretty simple, HIV: Sex acts that expose you to his semen and/or blood are definitely unsafe, and sex acts that expose him to your semen and/or blood are mostly safe. Rimming you, blowing you (even without a condom), getting fucked by you (with a condom)—all very low risk for HIV transmission. If he's on a drug regimen and his viral load is undetectable, HIV, your already-low risks of being exposed while, say, accepting a blowjob (and a check) are even lower. The risks aren't nonexistent—all sex acts carry some degree of risk—but if the risks were any closer to nonexistent, they'd be sitting on nonexistent's lap.

And bear this in mind: Odds are good that some of the other guys you've babied for—some of your previous daddies—were HIV positive and either didn't know or didn't have the decency to disclose.

This guy's willingness to disclose is evidence not just of his honesty and decency, HIV, but of his respect for you and his commitment to keeping you safe. This guy is less likely to ask you to engage in sex acts that are higher risk or unsafe than a guy who isn't aware that he's positive or is actively hiding the fact that he's positive. And his interest in being "used and abused" creates lots of hot safe-sex-play options—letting him beat off while he licks your boots or jerking him off while he's tied to the bed with your jock in his mouth are no-risk sexual activities that he's likely to enjoy immensely.

I'M A YOUNG LESBIAN. *I recently met a girl who's cute, and I think we're on the likely-to-have-sex-soon track. The thing is, she confided in me that she's participated in needle play in dungeon-party situations. I'm not someone who is turned off by kinkiness just 'cause it's kinky, but it seems like even "safe" needle play is a recipe for STI transmission unless you're playing with trained medical professionals. She says she gets tested regularly, but still, would it be really risky for me to sleep with her?*

Enthusiastic Reader

Every time I've watched needle play in a dungeon-party situation—watched with my hands clamped over my eyes, peeking through the small spaces between my fingers—no one was being stuck with rusty needles by dirty-handed brutes. All the public needle-play scenes I've witnessed were ostentatiously sterile affairs: These kinksters, some of whom were trained medical professionals, made

a big show of using alcohol wipes, cotton swabs, latex gloves, and clean sharps. I think it's fair to ask this girl for more information about her blood and needle experiences, about the safety precautions that her partners took, and about how recently she was tested. But rest assured, ER, that the most effective STI transmission routes involve sticking dicks in people in completely vanilla situations, not clean needles in dungeon-party situations.

I AM A 22-YEAR-OLD BISEXUAL MALE *who goes to a small, prestigious liberal-arts college in the Midwest. I've had boyfriends, girlfriends, and one-night stands, but I have never really felt like sex worked out as well as I imagine it could. I have a dominant personality, and people tend to follow me. Perhaps for this reason, I have fetishized submission. I imagine I would be into bondage and domination. I think I am a bit more attracted to women and would love to find a woman who takes a strong, dominant role in our relationship. I feel like I am always expected to make the first move with women, which has led me to prefer hooking up with men. I just wonder if there is anything I could do to find a woman who'd be into dominating me.*

I don't really like making the first move, but I've found just waiting and looking pretty doesn't work too well with women. Are there some ladies I could approach, and after the initial flirting, the dynamic would change and they would take the lead? How would I know who these people are?

Not Sure What I Want

There may be one or two young women kicking around your small, prestigious liberal-arts college who fantasize about taking the lead, about tying up and dominating their boyfriends, NSWIW, but they're not going to be tottering around campus in high-heeled boots and latex and leather. And even dominant women who are out tend to observe/succumb to the same cultural norms/practices that you find frustrating, i.e., they expect the male to make the first move, even in kinky environments.

But back to the young women you're likely to encounter at your prestigious college: A lot of women with naturally dominant and/or sadistic streaks—women who will one day really enjoy BDSM— don't realize it until that first submissive boyfriend draws it out of them. So if you want to get tied up, pegged, and bossed around while you're at college, NSWIW, you need to be paradoxically assertive about your submissive tendencies. You may have to ask four or five girls, or a dozen, before you hit the jackpot (before you ask a dominant girl), but you will have to take the lead.

MY BOYFRIEND AND I *have been together for nine months. We are gay. We live in a college town. We both found jobs here after we graduated, so we stayed. Since his sophomore year, my boyfriend has had an "arrangement" with an older man, a professor at the university. Did I say older? I meant old. We are in our mid-20s; this man is in his late 60s. The old man comes to my boyfriend's apartment once a week and cleans it. Does his laundry. Washes his dishes. He actually pays my boyfriend for the privilege. It's*

not much, $50, and the old perv says it's for my boyfriend's "time,"
since a part of their deal is that my boyfriend has to be in the
apartment while the old perv cleans it. He's particularly pervy
about how he cleans my boyfriend's bathroom. Dan, the old perv
cleans my boyfriend's toilet bowl with his own toothbrush, which
he then uses to brush his teeth the rest of the week!

There is no sex. (Presumably, the old perv goes home and beats
off after cleaning my boyfriend's apartment.) None of this would
matter if my boyfriend and I weren't talking about moving in
together. I want this "arrangement" to stop. I don't feel comfortable
using a toilet that a man old enough to be my grandfather cleaned
with his toothbrush. This has been going on for six years—since
my boyfriend was living in student housing. My boyfriend says
he likes the clean apartment more than he needs the money (and
that's true, now that he's no longer a starving student). But I say
all good things must come to an end, and if I'm moving in, we'll
have to clean up after ourselves or pay a real cleaning lady, like
regular people.

We agreed to leave it up to you. Dan: The old perv stays? The
old perv goes?

Toothbrushes Are For Teeth

The old perv stays.

By allowing this man to clean his apartment, TAFT, your
boyfriend is making an old perv very, very happy, and that makes
the world a more joyful place generally (and your boyfriend's

apartment a tidier place particularly). Your boyfriend isn't taking advantage of the old perv—$50 is a much more reasonable fee than most sex workers would charge for the same service (yes, your boyfriend is doing very low-level sex work)—and while the toothbrush/toilet thing is a bit . . . creepy . . . and unsanitary . . . I'm sure you'll get used to it and/or be able to put it out of your mind. (Although I'd be giving the toilet an additional wipe-down if anyone—young, old, hot, not—were cleaning it for me with a ratty old toothbrush.)

Let's recognize this arrangement for what it really is: a successful long-term relationship. How many relationships—gay or straight, monogamous or open, where toilets are scrubbed weekly with toothbrushes or cleaned sporadically with toilet brushes—last six years! Sorry, TAFT, but I'm constitutionally disinclined to dissolve a successful six-year relationship in favor of a relationship that has yet to reach the one-year mark.

And I think you knew, TAFT. I think you knew I would side with the perv—was there ever any question?—which leads me to believe that you're secretly okay with this arrangement and an extra $50 a week to put toward household expenses, money that you can invest in cases of Clorox Wipes. You wanted a little plausible deniability, a way for the arrangement to continue without having to give it your blessing, and needed some cover. And now you have it, TAFT.

I AM A 19-YEAR-OLD STRAIGHT MALE *who is only attracted to chubby girls, though I myself am rather skinny. It took a while,*

but I've learned to embrace this (though at first it seemed almost as scary as if I were to come out as gay). However, the problem I seem to have now is that the girls whom I find attractive—big girls—don't think of themselves as attractive, and that is a turnoff for me. Despite what seems like constant effort on my part to raise my exes' confidence in themselves, they never got any better and the relationships always ended. I'm not exactly bursting with confidence myself, either, but I tried my best to be a loving and supportive boyfriend. Yet time and time again, their images of themselves somehow seemed to actually turn worse, not better. I attribute a lot of their initial insecurity to the media, but I can't help but believe I somehow screw up and exacerbate it.

Troubled Horndog In Need

You're young and you've accepted your attraction to bigger girls, THIN, and that's great. But the girls you've dated—presumably close to your age—are doubtless still struggling with all the shit that's been thrown at them about their bodies. To grow confident about something that caused you a lot of pain—to say nothing of being with someone who's attracted to you in large part because of that something—can take time.

That said, THIN, if all the bigger girls you've dated emerged from your relationship feeling worse about themselves and their bodies . . . you might be doing something wrong. Were you treating your girlfriends like human beings and talking about their bodies in a way that made them feel attractive? Or did you treat them like fetish objects?

I'M A 20-YEAR-OLD GAY MALE *and I entered into a relationship with a guy at the beginning of the summer. The sex has always been really good, but I'm worried about pleasing him. He disclosed early on that he has a foot fetish. Sex usually consists of him topping me while sucking my toes or me jerking him off while he's fondling the bottoms of my feet. I don't have any problem with him getting off to my feet. My problem with the whole ordeal is this: I don't know diddly about foot fetishism. I tried Google, but my results weren't much better than "Foot fetishism is the most common form of sexual fetishism from an otherwise nonsexual object or body part, and it's different depending on who you're fucking." Not very helpful.*

I've talked to my boyfriend about what I can do to make things better and what he likes, but he's so bashful about the subject that I haven't gotten any information save "I prefer the soles of your feet." I have tried experimenting with things like footjobs (which didn't work out very well because I had no idea what I was doing), and not knowing what else to do is frustrating.

I am currently studying in France until the end of August, and I want to surprise him with my newfound knowledge on his kink and new ways to get him off. What should I know? What would you recommend? And could you fill me in on proper footjob technique?

Seeking Orgasm-Level Escalation

Male foot fetishists—the straight ones, anyway—will tell you that they react to feet the way most straight guys react to tits: aroused

by the sight of 'em, want to do stuff to 'em. Some wanna suck 'em, some wanna fuck 'em, and some kinksters wanna safely, sanely, and consensually "torture" 'em. In other words, SOLE, it's different depending on who the woman with the tits in question happens to be fucking.

Same goes for foot fetishists: Some wanna suck 'em, some wanna fuck 'em, some wanna "torture" 'em. (That's called "bastinado," and it should only be done safely, sanely, and consensually.) To find out what a particular foot fetishist enjoys most, you'll have to ask the foot fetishist who's enjoying your feet.

Your boyfriend probably finds it hard to talk about his fetish because he feels ashamed, needlessly so, and may have been rejected or mocked by previous partners when he opened up about his kink. (To avoid making his bashfulness worse, SOLE, avoid using terms like "problem" and "ordeal" when discussing his kink.) It's possible that the stuff you're doing for him now—sticking your toes in his mouth while he fucks you, jerking him off while he fondles your feet—fulfills all of his fantasies. Keep doing what you're doing now, SOLE, and as his confidence levels about his kink and your relationship both grow, he'll become less bashful about discussing his kink.

As for a proper footjob: Bring the bottoms of your feet together and let him fuck the gap between your soles with his lubed-up cock, titty-fucking style, or have him lie on the floor while you sit on the edge of the bed and move the lubed-up sole of one of your feet back and forth across his cock until he blows his load. Have fun!

So I'm in This Relationship and Something About the Sex Just Isn't Right

MY BOYFRIEND ALWAYS GOES SOFT *after he penetrates me. He's come in me only a handful of times—and I'm a bottom! When it comes to oral, he doesn't have trouble staying hard. Even more curious: The guy is only 21! Can someone that young really have "erectile dysfunction"? We've tried cock rings, and they don't help: He can keep his hard-on for a little longer (enough time to get inside me without getting soft), but it doesn't take long for him to get soft again. Dan, what do you think is going on? He'll be super-hard when I'm sucking him off, then I'll start jerking him a bit, then he'll get inside me, and then a very short while later he's soft. Is there anything we can do? Does he have ED?*

Lover Is Missing Poundings

Your boyfriend is hard during oral sex and when you jerk his cock, LIMP, and only loses his erection when he's in your ass or about to go in. Hmm. That doesn't sound like ED to me—there's no such thing as "act-specific ED"—but more like YBDLAS, or "your boyfriend doesn't like anal sex."

Your boyfriend may feel pressure to perform, LIMP, as being fucked is important to you. (Please tell me that he's coming inside a condom when he comes inside you.) And he may feel some pressure to conform. Anal sex among gay men has been elevated

to the status of vaginal sex among straight men, LIMP, in that it's somehow become the defining sex act, despite the fact that roughly a quarter of all gay men don't enjoy and don't indulge in anal sex. Your boyfriend may be one of those guys, but he's too inhibited to tell you how he feels because, hey, it's buttfucking and he's gay and all gay men are buttfuckers and if he doesn't enjoy buttfucking then he's some sort of defective gay buttfucker.

Tell him he doesn't have to do it if he doesn't enjoy it and, for the time being at least, you're taking anal off the menu—lifting the pressure off his shoulders and dick. Focus on the stuff that works for him right now: oral and JO. And remember, LIMP, if he's coming in your mouth, he's still coming inside you.

I MET MY GIRLFRIEND *about three months ago on a social-networking website. The pictures made her look attractive and in shape. We texted each other nonstop for the first three months. This past weekend we met, and she didn't look anything like her pictures. However, we did still have sex twice. I'm about to start my freshman year in college, and I do not want to be tied down going into school. Breaking up with her will break her heart into pieces. I have no clue what I should do.*

Epic State Of Confusion

You didn't meet your girlfriend three months ago, ESOC, you met this girl last weekend. And if she expects a lifetime commitment after posting misleading photos and exchanging text messages

and a single weekend of sex, she isn't just asking to have her heart broken, her heart *needs* breaking. So you'll have to break it for her, ESOC, unless you're prepared to be with this woman for the next six or seven decades.

She'll conclude that the breakup has something to do with her looks, of course, and that fact will make your rejection hurt all the worse. Good. She set herself up for rejection when she posted misleading photographs on that social-networking website and forged an emotional connection with you under what amounts to false pretenses. Your rejection may convince her to post more-representative photos—honest photos—in the future.

Anyone looking for sex partners online is free, of course, to post misleading photos of mysterious provenance. But those who do this have no one to blame for their hurt feelings but themselves. If I may paraphrase the caption under a famous *New Yorker* cartoon: On the internet, no one knows—or has to know—that you're a dog. But when chatting becomes cyberdating, when romance may be in the offing, and a face-to-face meeting becomes inevitable, an exchange of better photos—or at least more-representative photos—is simple common sense and common courtesy.

And here's where you went wrong, ESOC: You fucked this girl. She naturally interpreted your willingness to fuck her as a sign that you didn't care about the discrepancy between her photos and her actual appearance. It's going to make the rejection she has coming more devastating than it needed to be.

WHAT DOES A PERSON DO *when an LTR starts to feel stagnant or boring or dull?*

Partnered But Jonesing

A person experiments (with partner), cheats (on partner), or breaks up (with partner).

So I Think I Just Cheated

I LOVE MY BOYFRIEND OF THREE YEARS, *but I fucked up. We've had our ups and downs—he broke up with me for two months last summer because he said he was "young and needs to feel free"—but we've always worked through things. He is super supportive of me, and we've both really grown a lot as people together. But despite the affection and love, I just don't feel wanted. I don't feel like he wants to fuck my brains out like he used to. In fact, he rarely does, even when I try to initiate sex. Over the last six months, I've struggled with depression and not feeling sexy, and not feeling wanted is making both things worse. Last year, we talked about opening up our relationship, but I wasn't really comfortable with it.*

Long story short, I went to visit a friend in another city who lives practically next door to a former fling of mine from four years ago, and I ended up fooling around with the former fling. It wasn't full sex, but it was highly inappropriate. And yet . . . it felt so good to be wanted so badly.

I feel like a terrible person for so many reasons. I told my boyfriend—he didn't respond emotionally, and after 45 minutes he got up and left and said he would call me when he knew how he felt. I want him to forgive me, but I have a feeling he can't. I don't want to cause him any more pain than I already have, but I have no idea how to do that. Do I give him space? Do I go on with my life?

Self-Loathing Unfaithful Tramp

Go on with your life, SLUT. Suicide seems a little drastic, given the circumstances, so let's not open a vein over this.

It seems to me that the boyfriend was causing you a great deal of pain before you caused him pain. He has essentially rejected you again and again—the time he broke things off so he could "feel free" (what are you, a cage?), and the many times he's rejected you sexually and made you feel unwanted. Your sexual and emotional needs were not being met, and you succumbed to the attentions of a man who made you feel wanted. And that was unfortunate, SLUT, but it wasn't entirely your fault. If the boyfriend wasn't sending you the mother of all mixed signals—doesn't want to leave you, doesn't want to fuck you—you would have been either single and free to fool around on that trip or not at all interested in fooling around because you were getting what you needed at home.

So feel a little bad about what you did—you were technically involved with someone else when you messed around with that former fling—but don't feel too bad. This relationship needed to end; it wasn't making either of you happy.

Think of it this way: You slammed your car into a brick wall and totaled the thing. But it was a lemon, SLUT, and now you're free to get yourself a new ride.

So I Think I Just Got Raped

I'M AN 18-YEAR-OLD STRAIGHT FEMALE. *Two nights ago, I went to a party. My ex-boyfriend was present, but my current boyfriend was not. I had several beers, and while I wasn't drunk, I was tipsy. I had to go to my car to get my cell phone, and my ex offered to accompany me. When we got to the car, he pushed me against the car and started making out with me. I tried to push him away and said, "No, I can't" several times. He kept trying to pull my pants down, and every time he did, I pulled them back up. He took his dick out and tried again to pull down my pants. I know it sounds stupid, but all I could get out were meek "nos" and "I can'ts." I was afraid of a confrontation because he and I have been friendly since we broke up. I eventually discontinued my attempts to pull my pants back up because I figured the easiest way to get out of this situation was to let him finish. He had sex with me. I wanted to cry the whole time, but as much as I wanted to scream, "Stop! Get the fuck off of me!" I couldn't get the words out.*

I called my boyfriend when I got home and told him what happened. He is angry because he thinks I had a part in it. I don't know how to make him understand how many times I said no and how at first I physically stopped my ex from taking my clothes off.

My boyfriend and I have been through a lot together, and we talked about getting married one day. I never wanted to cheat on him, and while I feel guilty about what happened, I think he's being harsh on me considering I succumbed to force.

I've apologized again and again, but I don't know how to make things right. I still don't want a confrontation with the ex. I just want to forget about him and never see him or speak to him again. I just want things to be okay again with my boyfriend. Is there anything I can do or say to make him understand?

Date Rape Engenders Awful Depression

Understand that you were raped, DREAD—date-ish raped, acquaintance-ish raped, gray-area-ish raped, blurry-booze-soaked-lines raped, and raped under circumstances that would make bringing charges a futile exercise. But raped. Your ex kept coming at you, and you were paralyzed by a set of inhibitions—a desire to avoid confrontation at all costs (even the cost of your own violation), a desire to avoid making your victimizer feel bad—that are pounded into the heads of girls and young women. Your ex exploited this vulnerability. Your ex may not think he raped you since you finally "let him," and perhaps he interprets that as consent and so, distressingly, does your boyfriend. But raped you were.

So what do you do now? I'd suggest a bit more contact with your ex. You need to confront him—for your own sake, DREAD, but also for the sake of all other women he's going to encounter over the course of his life. If you can't face him, call him. If you can't speak

to him, write him. Wherever he is right now, he's rationalizing away his responsibility for what happened. He may be telling himself that he was drunk, that you were drunk, and that, sure, he may have been aggressive at first, but that you came around and enjoyed it as much as he did. He needs to hear from you that you regard—and, for what it's worth, I regard—what happened as rape. Tell him that he didn't get away with it—that he raped you, you know it, and now he knows it. Then tell him that if the circumstances were just a little less ambiguous, DREAD, that you would be going to the police.

Hell, tell him you still might. Put the fear of god into him.

Then you need to confront the boyfriend: If your boyfriend can't take your side, DREAD, if he can't see what really happened here, if he insists on victimizing you, too, then you don't need him in your life any more than you need your ex in your life.

So I Think I'm Pregnant

I WAS HANGING OUT WITH A GUY *who is in a relationship. I told him nothing could happen, and we decided to keep things friendly. A while ago, I made the drunken mistake of climbing into the backseat of a car with him (elegant, I know). Things got racy pretty quickly, mostly a bunch of making out and touching, but then he asked if I was on birth control. I told him yes, because I was, and he penetrated me and came inside of me after one thrust.*

The next day, I got all emotional about our situation in relation to his relationship, and OMG what kind of girl does he think I am

now, and blah blah blah. He's since stopped talking to me because I freaked. Here we are a bit later, and I just had a pregnancy scare. Had I been pregnant, I would have had an abortion. If I'd actually been facing an abortion, I would have called and told him. Would that have been the right thing to do?

I wouldn't have asked for money or support; I would have told him solely because it would have felt wrong not to. I had some feeling, like he should know—because he has a right to know, you know? I can't imagine I'm the only woman who's been faced with a "to tell or not to tell" situation. Weigh in?

Classy Lady

A woman who is pregnant and has decided to have an abortion should tell the guy who knocked her up about the pregnancy and her decision to abort—unless she sincerely believes—or even legitimately suspects—that the guy is gonna bully, badger, and/or do violence to her in an attempt to prevent her from choosing abortion.

Guys need to know when they've dodged a bullet, CL. Being made aware that he came this close to 18 years' worth of child support payments can lead a guy to be more cautious with his spunk—and, in some cases, more likely to support choice.

Take the guy you fucked: He needs to know that not all birth control methods are foolproof and not every woman who claims to be on birth control is telling the truth and/or being diligent about taking those pills every day. Hearing that almost-a-daddy bullet

whiz past his head may convince him to put on that condom the next time he's fucking a woman he isn't serious about, even if she is (or claims to be) on birth control.

And . . . um . . . gee. This bit is going to get me scratched off NARAL's Christmas card list, which will be a real bummer (last year's card was great: "The Crusades, the Inquisition, clerical sex-abuse scandals—all of this could have been prevented. Happy holidays from your friends at NARAL"), but I gotta be me. A guy—a good, decent, nonabusive guy—should be told about an impending abortion so he can, if he feels the abortion is a mistake, make a case for keeping the baby. It's still the woman's choice in the end—there should be absolutely no question about that—but the fetus, if not the uterus, is his, too. It's only fair that the same guy who would be on the hook for child support payments if you decide to go through with the pregnancy be heard out before you follow through on your decision to end it.

So I Think I'm Trans

. . . .

I HAVE BEEN CONSIDERING BECOMING A WOMAN. *But the straight women I have talked to about this are very reluctant to assist me in my transition from being male to being female. I am wondering if you think that lesbians might be more open-minded in assisting me in my transition.*

Gender Identity Readjustment Looming

You're considering becoming a woman—that's wonderful, GIRL, very interesting, very compelling stuff, always a special time in a man's life. But it's not like you're rushing a sorority; current members—the straight women you've approached, the lesbians you're thinking about approaching—are not obligated to answer your questions, offer you assistance, host a tea, or take even the slightest interest in your transition. Find a support group for MTFs, GIRL, and you'll find plenty of women—longtime members and new pledges—interested in hearing about your journey. But leave the women you meet in the normal course of your life—straight women and lesbians who are not your friends—alone.

I'M A 22-YEAR-OLD FTM. *I will become a legal male this summer. WOOT. Useless hole but still no pole. My friends—all straight—don't know because I don't feel it matters. I don't know any other FTMs, and I really don't care to. However, I like men. I have never had a boyfriend. I go to gay clubs, flirt, dance, and make out with other gay men. But when I am up front about being FTM, I never hear from a guy again. My question is, when do I tell a gay man I have been flirting with that I am not a bio male? I don't want to deceive them, but I at least want a chance for them to get to know me first.*

No Pole, No Go

The first thing Buck Angel—trans activist, public speaker, and porn star—wanted to say, NPNG, was congrats in advance on becoming

a legal male. The second thing Buck wanted to say was that hole of yours isn't useless.

"If he isn't familiar with my work, maybe he should check it out," said Buck (www.buckangel.com). "I get tremendous pleasure from my hole. Whether a transman plans on getting a penis or not, there still has to be a time that he realizes that what's between his legs does not define who he is."

It seems to me that time—the time you realized that you're not defined by what's between your legs—had to have come before you began transitioning, NPNG, otherwise you wouldn't be transitioning. As for how the guys you're meeting in gay bars feel about what is or isn't between your legs, Buck has some advice for you about that, too: "If he meets a guy and tells him about himself—which is the right thing to do—and he doesn't hear back, then that wasn't the right guy for him."

If you're not having any luck with messy face-to-face meetings/make-out sessions in gay bars, Buck suggests you consider online dating.

"If he's looking to hook up," said Buck, "here's a site where he can start: www.ftmlover.com. He'll see that there are tons—and I mean TONS—of men out there who are interested in guys like us!"

But before you start meeting those guys, NPNG, Buck thinks—and I agree—that you have to become more comfortable in your own skin. "Be proud of your body," said Buck. "When you feel confident that you are a man, no one can tell you otherwise."

And do you know what might help you feel more confident? Getting to know some other trans guys.

"There are many reasons that someone might isolate themselves from other trans and gay people," said Ezra Goetzen, a mental health therapist and trans community activist. "Some folks identify as male-to-male, seeing their transition as a medical procedure rather than a path to a transgender identity. Others, due to the fabulously flattering cultural/media images of trans people in general, internalize the shame, indifference, and disgust—and they don't want to be reminded of these feelings by hanging out with other trans people."

Whatever your particular reason for avoiding transmen, NPNG, you're doing yourself a disservice.

"Being isolated from other trans folks leaves little room to find support and role models for loving yourself," said Goetzen. "And it makes getting invaluable tips on how to get laid safely and carefully harder."

So I'm a Virgin—Or My Partner Is

I'M A 21-YEAR-OLD, GOOD-LOOKING, *sexually active, single woman. I have never had a boyfriend, but I have many guy friends who tell me that I'm great. Is it that men don't want to date me, or is my lack of putting up with bullshit getting me into trouble?*

Alone Again Unnaturally

You don't give me much to work with here, AAU. For instance, examples of the kind of bullshit you're incapable of putting up with might help. Because you know what? Some bullshit is intolerable,

AAU, but there's no such thing as a bullshit-free relationship. A long-term relationship is, at its core, two people struggling to put up with each other's bullshit—day in, day out, year after year—in exchange for things intangible (love) and things tangible (sex). And why should anyone put up with your bullshit, kiddo, if you won't put up with theirs?

I'M 21, FEMALE, AND PRETTY EXPERIENCED. *The guy I'm dating now is 23 and a virgin. I'd really like to avoid some of the awkwardness that I'm sure is going to arise, seeing as I'm his first. (And has arisen—the first time we attempted to do the deed, he was so nervous he couldn't stay hard; he also thought he was "in" when, in reality, he was humping my leg.) I'm at a loss. Obviously this is going to take a lot of communication in the moment; aside from that, do you have any advice for how to make this less awkward for both of us?*

First Isn't Really Sexy Time

Mess around a few times—at least a half a dozen times—with vaginal penetration off the menu, ratcheting down the performance anxiety for your boy. Once he's seen that, yes, his dick does work—yes we can get hard, yes we can stay hard, yes we can blow a load with a woman in the room—then you can move on to vaginal intercourse. And take control, FIRST: Tell him—as sexily as possible—what you're going to do before you get started, tell him what you're doing while you're doing it, and then you can tell him when he's "in" instead of letting him guess.

And, finally, a little required reading for the virgins out there

and the people who are about to fuck some sense into them: *The Virgin Project.* Illustrators K. D. Boze and Stasia Kato interviewed all sorts of people—gay, straight, bi; young, old, ancient—about their loss-of-virginity experiences. The illustrated stories in *The Virgin Project* are moving, hilarious, and heartbreaking in turn—sometimes all three at once—and knowing that everyone's first time is awkward, and that some folks' first times are unpleasant, and that most of us survive them, might be good for your virgin, FIRST. It couldn't hurt you to be reminded of those things, either.

I'M 19 YEARS OLD AND GAY AND A VIRGIN. *Now I've met a guy I kind of like. He's hot, great body. He wanted to fuck me, to be my first, the night we met, but I'm not sure I want to have anal sex. He insisted that we didn't need to use a condom, since I'm a virgin and he's "clean," and got kind of upset when I tried to say no. I'm going to see him again, and I don't think I'll be able to make the same excuse again. (I told him I wasn't feeling "empty" enough to do it that night.) What do I say to get him to use condoms? I don't want to drive him off, because he's really hot. But I don't want to be unsafe or get HIV or even have anal sex right now.*

Just Out Newbie

I've covered this issue before, JON—but, gee, the last time I answered a letter from a gay kid in your situation was, um, when

you were 12. But the advice I gave Bright Kid, Big City back then still applies now, so here it goes:

Look, JON, any faggot who wants to fuck you in the ass without a condom is the LAST PERSON ON EARTH you should be having sex with—anal or otherwise, condoms or no condoms. Guys who pressure you into having sex without condoms are having or have had unsafe sex with other people, which means that they're either infected already or will be shortly. If you don't want to get infected, your best course of action when a guy pressures you into having sex without condoms—or any kind of sex you're not comfortable with—is to pull up your pants and leave.

And since you're not particularly interested in anal sex right now, JON, I'd urge you to tell the guys you do go home with that you're just not up for getting fucked. An aversion to anal sex when you're young and just out and easily manipulated is something you should hold on to, JON, even cultivate. Skipping anal sex during your great-big-slut, just-coming-out, making-your-mistakes phase will greatly reduce your risk of contracting HIV and a host of other STIs. Then one day, with luck, you'll meet a nice, decent guy, also hot, who wants to take things slow—a guy who isn't a manipulative, selfish, barebacking piece of shit. And when you meet that guy, JON, you can explore anal with someone who cares about you enough to take it slow and wear condoms.

Anal sex, despite the impression created by HIV "prevention" materials you may have encountered, should not be a first-date activity. Reserve your asshole for guys you're serious about, JON,

and for guys who are serious about you. The hot motherfucker you're seeing right now isn't worthy. Walk away.

I AM A STRAIGHT, 18-YEAR-OLD GIRL *and a college freshman. A couple of months ago, I lost my virginity to my first serious boyfriend, and since then we've been having sex several times a day. Apparently we have been a bit too enthusiastic, because my boyfriend received a note from his downstairs neighbors. In crass and abusive language, they told us to keep it down. I was mortified. Post-note, I've been tense and nervous during sex, more focused on listening for the neighbors than enjoying the act. This is upsetting me terribly, and I don't know how to make it better. Even if we are both silent, the bed inevitably squeaks and thumps. There is really nowhere else on campus for us to go (I have three roommates who don't get out much). What should I do? I am so depressed by this situation.*

Loud And Clear

Go buy the original Broadway cast recording of *Avenue Q*. The next time you have sex, blast "You Can Be as Loud as the Hell You Want (When You're Makin' Love)" at top volume. When the neighbors complain about the music, tell them that they can listen to show tunes or put up with the noise you guys make when you have sex—their pick.

7. WHAT NO ONE ELSE WILL TELL YOU ABOUT DRINKING

BY BETHANY JEAN CLEMENT

Since the first velociraptor ate the first fermented prehistoric cherry-things, creatures have taken pleasure in intoxication by way of beautiful, beautiful alcohol. That being said, it's true that all things should be enjoyed in moderation—including moderation, which means that from time to time, you'll want to get properly drunk. Very good! Let's just don't be too stupid about it. Onward!

How to Deal With a Hangover

You poor thing! Here, take these Advil and drink some water. Go back to bed or watch a soothing movie. Drink some more water; you're dehydrated. When you're ready, locate some bland, preferably greasy food and eat it.

You still feel like total hell exhumed from a place worse than death and oh my god your head and why isn't there such a thing as a tongue transplant and WHY DID YOU SAY THAT ONE THING if in fact you can even remember that one thing you said? Take it easy; everybody's been there. The bad news, aside from your crushing hangover, is that you're just going to have to wait your crushing hangover out.

People have sought relief from the aftereffects of overindulgence in our friend alcohol since the first caveman made some prison-style brew, and no one's found anything truly efficacious yet. Some swear by the spicy Mexican soup menudo, or pho with lots of sriracha hot sauce in it, but they're just as likely to irritate your already very irritated stomach. Sports drinks and vitamins might help a little, or that might just be placebo effect. If you'd thought about it last night, you could've alternated one alcoholic drink with one water all night, which does work, but probably only by slowing you down (in large part because you're spending so much time in the bathroom), but it's not last night anymore, is it? OH GOD, LAST NIGHT.

A little caffeine—not a lot—could make you feel slightly less horrible. (Plus water! Always more water!) A small amount of the

proverbial hair of the dog that bit you—that is, alcohol—might assist with launching you into a restorative nap (same with a little bit of pot). But more than that, and you're looking to get bit again by the dog that already bit you whose hair you just drank.

British novelist Kingsley Amis maintained that a hangover could be helped by either (1) a half-hour flight in an open-air plane or (2) vigorous sex. If you have the opportunity for either (or both), you should clearly take it—though he rightfully cautions against option 2 "if you are in bed with somebody you should not be in bed with, and have in the least degree a bad conscience about this." You will want to acquire a copy of *Everyday Drinking*, Amis' collected works on the topic written between 1971 and 1984. The essay "The Hangover" addresses both the physical and the metaphysical aspects of the situation, the latter of which he terrifyingly yet encouragingly describes as "the psychological, moral, emotional, spiritual aspects: all that vast, vague, awful, shimmering metaphysical superstructure that makes the hangover a (fortunately) unique route to self knowledge and self realisation." Here you will further find helpful recommendations for reading and music that may enable the embetterment of the hungover soul (as well as a consideration of Kafka's *The Metamorphosis* as a metaphor for the hangover).

Some people swear by Alka-Seltzer, but good lord, does it taste terrible.

The internet reports that an old Irish remedy for a hangover was to bury the hungover person up to the neck in moist river sand.

However, if a body of water such as a river happens to be at hand, brief immersion in it is clearly superior to burial of whatever kind.

Drinking a glass or two of water (but not a lot more) before you go to bed is a good idea.

But in the end, like a broken heart (see How to Get Over a Broken Heart, page 212), a hangover can only truly be mended by the passage of time. Meanwhile, more water, more ibuprofen (though take it easy—you could end up with damage to your insides), more rest, some food. Don't torture yourself about the stupid things you did or said; it happens to the best of us. There, there. This too shall pass. Until next time.

How to Binge Drink

It must be said: Binge drinking is not a great idea. You could get raped; you could fall out a window; you could die of alcohol poisoning or aspirating your own vomit. You ought not to do it, but if you do, best to do it as safely and non-jackassly as possible.

Good friends with whom to binge drink are of paramount importance, as is being explicit about what being a good friend in this circumstance means (including but not limited to: preventing predatory characters from luring a friend away; moving a friend away from any open windows near which they are teetering; putting a passed-out friend to bed on their side—not their back or front—then checking on them; not putting a passed-out friend in a

cold shower, as the friend may die of shock; calling 911 if a friend is dry-heaving without stopping).

While the goal may be obliteration, a little self-awareness along the way helps immensely: Are those around you enjoying you as much as you're enjoying yourself? Is the lampshade on your head completely necessary? Are you about to vomit? (If so, see On Vomiting, page 120.)

Skip the mid-drinking-binge marijuana (same goes for the bedtime bong hit): It will very likely have an emetic effect. Drink some water (though your hangover is inevitable—plan for it). At bedtime, if you get the spins, hang one leg out of bed, foot touching the floor.

And know when to say when, even with excess: If you binge drink frequently over a long period of time, get some help. If your relationships/schoolwork/work/life suffers because of your drinking—if you can't make it to class or miss shifts, if your friends tell you that you have a problem, if your significant other wants to dump you—ditto.

Handy Synonyms for Being Drunk

Hammered, schnockered, wasted, blitzed, bombed, blotto, buzzed, trashed, canned, loaded, smashed, soused, sloshed, tanked, tight, tipsy, inebriated, intoxicated, in your cups, three sheets to the wind, liquored up, lit, all lashed up (chiefly British), wrecked, plastered.

On Vomiting

It's only human: Sometimes people barf. Drinking, especially in a purposeful fashion—doing shots, playing beer pong, or just really applying yourself to the alcohol at hand—increases the chances of hurling. Vomiting isn't bad, per se; it's just your body's way of saying, "HEY, FRIEND! YOU'RE POISONING ME!" And it's true: Once you puke, you'll feel better.

But! You don't want to be That Person: the one who spewed in the middle of the dance floor, or in somebody's car, or on someone's feet, especially if they're wearing sandals. If you feel like you're about to throw up, heed that feeling and act immediately. Your time is limited, and hemming and hawing just increases your chances of problematic regurgitation. This is no time to stand on ceremony: The most polite thing you can do is spare others the horror of seeing and smelling what you're about to do. No need to excuse yourself; just go! Get to the nearest restroom or get outside, away from others—then have at it. (If you're in a car, don't be shy; the driver would much, much rather pull over than deal with the interior aftermath.) Ugh! But wait: That's better, isn't it? And no one thinks you're an asshat.

If you feel woozy, don't lie down in the locked bathroom or shrubbery; get back around other people, and tell your friends about your predicament. It is their job to make sure you don't pass out on your back and choke to death. Not to put too fine a point on it, but no one wants to find you dead in a pool of your own vomit later.

If you feel SO MUCH BETTER, well, good on ya! Some stalwart people have been known to celebrate by drinking more (a.k.a. the boot-and-rally). If that's you, you're now firmly in binge-drinking territory. No judgment! But do see How to Binge Drink, page 118.

Handy Synonyms for Vomiting

Throw up, barf, puke, hurl, spew, retch, regurgitate, disgorge, de-food, ride the porcelain bus, pray to the porcelain god, do the Technicolor yawn, liquid laughter, hot liquid breath, chunder, heave, hork, honk (chiefly British), toss a pavement pizza, upchuck, blow chunks, boot, lose your cookies, lose your lunch, whistle a solid tune.

How to Get Roofied and Still Have a Good Time

The key to enjoying getting roofied is good company. If you're drinking at a party or a bar, you should already be with a friend or friends who understand, seriously, how to look after each other (see How to Binge Drink, page 118). You should be keeping an eye on each other's drinks, too—and no setting it down and coming back to it, dummy, or accepting a drink from the hand of someone you don't know. If you somehow do get roofied, then your wingperson or -people are there to fend off (and hopefully punch) whatever creep tries to drag you off into the night. (As a human being, it's also your duty to always watch for creeps dragging other half-conscious

people off into the night: Stop them and yell, "Do you know her? WHAT THE FUCK, DUDE?" until the situation is made very clear.) With your friends by your side, you can relax and experience whatever psychotropic substance has been introduced into your system, which might not be that bad—some have reported crystal-clear double vision accompanied by fits of laughter, with only a small amount of blacking-out later (with friends to keep watch—see how that works?).

How to Drink Like an Adult

One's introduction to alcohol often involves kegs and keg-stands and shots and putting it up your butt (is that really a thing? Do you really want to find out?). Oh, the fun! We mean that. But there comes a time to put away childish things (while noting that you can always come back to them later) and drink like an adult. Such a time might include a first date, when one thing not to do is offer them a funnel in the movie-theater parking lot; or dinner with someone's parents, when one thing not to do is propose a round of Jäger; or, at some point, the entire rest of your life. (You will maybe regress to play beer pong just once in a while. It will be surprisingly fun.) Here's how.

Do not order a rum-and-Coke. Do not order a Diet-and-anything. Do not drink anything that is pink or anything that is blended. Do not drink malt liquor or schnapps of any variety. Do not drink anything containing flecks of gold, or taurine, or caffeine.

Do not order any drink that has more than three components; two components are preferable (for the exception to this rule, see Why Do the Drinks at This Bar Cost So Goddamn Much?, page 126).

Tip your bartender. This means $1 per drink, minimum, every time. What??? You're already paying for the drink!!! And it's only a however-few-dollars beer!!!!! Ah, how right you are. However, you are now drinking like an adult, and an inviolable part of the social contract is that one drink equals one dollar in tippage (if not more). The good news is that if you tip well and say thank you, bartenders will quite often eventually buy you a round. See how that works?

Do not partake in any drinking that involves dropping one beverage into another. Do not do shots. While drinking games may have their pleasures, rest assured you are venturing out of the realm of adultlike drinking if dice, cards, coins, word-cues, elaborate hand gestures, or rules of any kind are involved. Do not gulp.

Drinking is the accompaniment to another activity, such as conversation or eating; drinking is not an activity unto itself. Do not say or do things that are dramatically different from the things you would say or do while not drinking. Do not cause difficulty for others due to your drinking, and do not let drinking cause difficulties for you. The only rules of adult drinking are more like guidelines, and they are ones that also apply to life as a whole: Don't get too complicated about it, and don't be an ass.

On Drinking and Driving

You're not better at it than other people. It is completely irrelevant that you're just going to the store, or whatever. DO. NOT. DO. IT.

Beer: It's All Good

One's path with our friend beer generally follows a certain trajectory: You have sips of beer as a kid and it tastes terrible; you drink crummy, cheap beer and it tastes terrible; you have more money and drink microbrews, and they are better; and maybe you venture into Belgian and other schmancy beers, and they taste even better, and you drink them sometimes, otherwise enjoying microbrews or even cheap beer (or variations thereof, such as Corona) when you want something that's just cold and refreshing. In extreme cases, you might start brewing your own beer and become a real beer geek, which is as good a hobby as any. The thing is, all beer is good beer; to each their own. Don't get too wound up about it.

Wine: What the Hell's the Deal?

One's path with our friend wine generally follows the same general trajectory we just discussed with our friend beer: At first, it just tastes gross; then you drink cheap wine, which also tastes gross; then you spring for something a little better, and yay for that; then maybe eventually you drift off into the ether of wine enthusiasm,

spending lots of money and using lots of insane adjectives and becoming more annoying by the minute (we once heard a wine described—seriously—as "like lathered ponies").

A thing to know is that the step up from grocery-store jug wine to, say, wine that's $10 a bottle is a worthwhile step. Assuming you're 21, go to a neighborhood wine shop and throw yourself on their mercy—tell them you have $10 to spend and that you want a crisp-tasting, dry white or a not-too-big red. (You can mess around with sweeter wines, or chardonnay, or cabernet, if you want—it's your life.) Trader Joe's has some decent stuff, too. Not to be unpatriotic, but conventional wisdom holds that lower-priced French or Spanish or Italian or South American wines are better than ours. After a while, you'll start getting an idea about what you like, and sometimes you'll spend a little more, and you'll be able to order wine at a restaurant, and it'll be neat.

Oh, wait! There's also rosé. For a long time, rosé was the redheaded stepchild of wine—sticky-sweet and bound to give you a headache. They're still pink, but rosés today are, by and large, refreshing summertime greatness. Moreover, $10 is a perfectly good amount to spend on a bottle of rosé (that's $2.50 a glass). Look for a lighter-colored rosé—the pretty peachy ones taste better than the bright-pink strumpets. Chill well, and enjoy outdoors if possible.

Why Do the Drinks at This Bar Cost So Goddamn Much?

Hey, wait a minute—there aren't any TVs at this bar. It's all old-fashionedy up in here, with duck decoys and shelves of ancient tomes and stuff! The bartenders are wearing old-timey garb like vests and ties. They seem so serious! Also, they are taking nearly literally forever to make each drink, which costs nearly literally one million dollars.

Congratulations and/or condolences, friend: You have found yourself on the vanguard of alcohol consumption, in the realm of the "craft cocktail." The name of the place probably has something to do with Prohibition (when ALCOHOL WAS ILLEGAL IN THESE HERE UNITED STATES OF AMERICA, for the 13 long years from 1920 to 1933, if you can fathom that), and it exists with the sole purpose of making you a complicated and expensive and probably very tasty drink. There aren't any blended margaritas, because they do not have a blender—they have a special stick for hand "muddling," among other arcane cocktail tools.

Here, you must first resign yourself to the price of your drink plus 20 percent—at these bars, you look like a shitheel if you tip less than 20 percent. Then you might ask to see the cocktail menu and choose something off it that sounds vaguely up your alley, or that just has a name you like, or completely at random. When these bartenders are good, they can make something that sounds horrifying taste like a liquid unicorn. If you want to up the ante,

you could ask what local spirits they particularly recommend, or whether the bar is making its own bitters or barrel-aged cocktails or shrub (it's a thing!). But watch out: You might find yourself quickly out of your depth, nodding while you get an earful of you know not what.

Perhaps the best tactic at the craft cocktail bar is to describe, very briefly, what you like—e.g., brown liquor (always brown liquor! These people will go around the bend if you ask for vodka!), bitter/sour rather than sweet, no orange flavors—and ask what they'd recommend. Say you want rye—they love that.

Cheers, friend.

8. WHAT NO ONE ELSE WILL TELL YOU ABOUT DRUGS

BY CHRISTOPHER FRIZZELLE, BRENDAN KILEY, AND DAVID SCHMADER

Don't Do Drugs! Okay? Seriously! Ever . . .

D rugs are illegal and dangerous, and you should never do them. They can destroy your brain, your nostrils, your future employment prospects, and your chance at happiness. Anyone who tries to tell you that drugs are no big deal is a drug dealer.

That said: WOO-HOO! College! The word practically *smells* like weed. We just wrote that first paragraph in case your grandma flips open to that page.

To reiterate, we're not telling you to try drugs.

But if you are going to try them anyway—and if you're anywhere near open-minded, you probably are—you deserve some no-bullshit information. And in a country seized by hysterical and exaggerated antidrug messaging from the government and your grandma, nonhysterical, nonexaggerated information about drugs is hard to come by. We came by this information the old-fashioned way: doing drugs. Some drugs will suit you better than others; some drugs that have a certain effect on everyone else will have the opposite effect on you. After all, individual metabolic and brain-chemical reactions vary widely. Take half a dose or less the first time you take anything, and see how it makes you feel.

If experience has taught us anything, it's that, as with anything worth doing, drugs demand moderation. Used habitually, any drug is habit-forming, and things you learn to do while high— study for exams, meet parents of boyfriends/girlfriends, survive the holidays—you'll be tempted to do high for the rest of your life. However, with proper care and restraint, collegiate drug experiments can be a source of enlightenment, entertainment, and adventure.

If you feel like you're going off the rails, don't hesitate to get help right away, and don't feel ashamed. Addiction isn't a moral failing—it's a roll of the genetic dice. And, as with most things in

life, it is far, far better to recognize a problem and deal with it than to let it fester. If you get too fucked-up too often, you will make yourself and the people who love you totally fucking miserable. Try to avoid that.

Here are some drug-specific pointers to help you find your way.

Marijuana

A.K.A.: Pot, potential, grass, weed, Mary Jane, 420, ganja, herb, chronic, coughy ha-ha.

METHOD OF INGESTION: Smoked, eaten.

EFFECTS: A warm, time-expanding fuzziness that amplifies the hilarity and deliciousness of everything.

SIDE EFFECTS: Short-term memory loss (never a good thing for students, since you're spending a lot of time and money cramming stuff into your brain), bottomless appetite, occasional paranoia.

FOR BEST RESULTS: Conduct initial experiments in a safe space free of stress and social obligation. If you find you enjoy pot, restrict usage to weekends, preferably late morning, en route to a pancake house or a matinee. Smoking pot during the week—going to class or doing homework stoned—is a surefire way to flunk your classes. When you're stoned, easy tasks become difficult, your professor's lectures will be impossible to follow, reading will be a challenge because you'll be much more absorbed in the shape of the letters on the page than in what the words are saying, and formulating complete thoughts of your own can be comically daunting.

In conversation, you will constantly forget what you were about to say, which is hilarious if you're sitting around with a good friend who already knows you're not an idiot, but is less hilarious if you're trying not to sound stupid in front of people you don't know very well. All that said, marijuana is one of those drugs whose downsides are dramatically exaggerated. It can be great for creativity, relaxation, and sex, and in several countries that have not fallen off the map, recreational marijuana use is not a crime. Marijuana also has documented medical benefits. It's great for chronic stomachaches and people with HIV and cancer, for example.

DO NOT: Take a hit of weed if you're drunk, or you'll get the spins and vomit.

ROMANTIC TIP: "Shotgunning" is when you exhale the smoke from your mouth into someone else's mouth. This requires your lips to touch theirs, also known as kissing. The shotgunnee does, indeed, also get high (if a little less so). Recycling works!

CEASE USAGE IF: You gain more than 20 pounds from munchie-induced gorging or you can't remember what you're supposed to remember.

Cocaine

A.K.A.: Blow, snow, coke, booger sugar, Mr. White, skiing, the rich man's life-ruiner.

METHOD OF INGESTION: Snorted. (If it's smoked or injected, it's called crack.)

EFFECTS: Temporary feeling of confidence, extreme loquaciousness, surging energy. Cocaine is a drinker's drug: When you're on it, you can drink and drink and not get tired.

SIDE EFFECTS: Deviated septum, crippling annoyingness, almost instant desire for more.

BE WARNED: Cocaine is cut with all kinds of poisons, including levamisole, a cattle-deworming drug that's shown up across the US drug supply in the last few years and that can rot your face off and obliterate your immune system. (To learn more about that, see www.thestranger.com/cocaine.) Cocaine is also funding the current bloodbath in Mexico, and regular use—whether snorting, smoking, or injecting—tends to harden people's souls, making them selfish, aggressive, rude, and worse at everything (academics, art, sports, empathy). Science doesn't have a satisfying answer for why that happens, but you will see it happen over and over again to anyone who takes a liking to cocaine.

FOR BEST RESULTS: Use once if you must, twice if you love it, three or more times if you want trouble.

CEASE USAGE IF: You're sleeping with dealers to support your habit. KIDDING! Way, way, way before that. Like now.

Methamphetamine

. . . .

A.K.A.: Crystal, meth, crystal meth, tina, crank, hillbilly crack, the poor man's life-ruiner.

METHOD OF INGESTION: Smoked, snorted, injected.

EFFECTS: Frazzled alertness, compulsive horniness, grossly inflated sense of self.

SIDE EFFECTS: Tooth loss, paranoia, insomnia, tremors, twitching, friendlessness, heart attack, stroke, death.

FOR BEST RESULTS: Run in the other direction.

CEASE USAGE IF: You're stupid enough to do it in the first place.

Ecstasy

....

A.K.A.: E, X, MDMA, Molly, happy-fun pills.

METHOD OF INGESTION: Swallowed.

EFFECTS: Four to six hours of ravishing happiness and emotional openness.

SIDE EFFECTS: Clenched teeth, severe day-after depression.

RECOMMENDED ACTIVITIES: Talking, dancing, touching, or being touched. Though some people view ecstasy as a sex drug, it can be difficult for men to get it up, which is a real damper on sexytime.

BE WARNED: If you're on antidepressants, you might not feel much, as many antidepressants regulate the amount of serotonin your brain will release at a time.

DON'T FORGET: Water. Ecstasy-related deaths are almost always the result of dehydration. But not too much water! A few fools have died of waterloggedness. (True!)

FOR BEST RESULTS: Use once a year for the duration of your college career.

CEASE USAGE IF: You're extending your college career so you can keep doing ecstasy.

LSD

A.K.A.: Acid, WHOA!!!!!

METHOD OF INGESTION: Absorbed on tongue.

EFFECTS: Fascinatingly fractalized experience of space and time, hallucinations.

SIDE EFFECTS: Sometimes-scary knowledge of the intimate workings of the universe.

FOR BEST RESULTS: Use with close friends, in nature, no more than once a year. Find a safe and comfortable place, eat a light, bland meal beforehand, and make sure you have lots of water as well as an experienced "lifeguard" who can help everyone stay safe and sane.

CEASE USAGE IF: You value your sanity.

Mushrooms

A.K.A.: Magic mushrooms, 'shrooms, funny fungus.

METHOD OF INGESTION: Eaten or drunk as tea.

EFFECTS: Kinda like LSD, but less intense, friendlier. Mushrooms are a college-druggie favorite, and like marijuana, they have the advantage of being produced in nature and not made in laboratories by people who don't care about you, like many other drugs. Depending on the dosage, setting, and your individual brain chemistry, mushrooms can crack open the universe and bring profound insights about the wholeness and beauty of everything, or send you barreling down a terrible tube of fear and anxiety.

SIDE EFFECTS: Similar to acid, with an extra risk of puking from the grossness of the mushrooms.

BE WARNED: Don't go out hunting for mushrooms on your own if you don't really, really know what you're doing. Scientists have only classified 15 percent of the world's fungi, and a lot of *known* fungi are deadly, to saying nothing of unknown fungi.

FOR BEST RESULTS: (See LSD.)

CEASE USAGE IF: (See LSD.)

Heroin

. . . .

A.K.A.: Smack, horse, dope, fentanyl (synthetic heroin), sweet lady H.

METHOD OF INGESTION: Snorted, smoked, injected.

EFFECTS: An avalanche of ravishing, full-body pleasure compressing a lifetime of orgasms into one hour-long rush.

SIDE EFFECTS: Puking, as well as almost instant enslavement to that avalanche of ravishing, full-body pleasure compressing a lifetime of orgasms into one hour-long rush. With enough time, opiates will turn pretty much anyone into a robot programmed exclusively for narcotic longing. Being addicted to opiates—from oxy to heroin—is like having each cell in your body suffering from both heartbreak and food poisoning. The short-term solution to the problem is more opiates. The long-term solution to the problem is powering through the misery of withdrawal. If you must use opiates, use them *very* sparingly and never, ever take them (recreationally) for two days in a row. That is the first step down a hallway that leads to metabolic

addiction, a condition you will not have noticed entering until you feel the first painful thrums of withdrawal shivering through your body. That is not a feeling you want to experience.

FOR BEST RESULTS: Stay away. Like crystal meth, heroin is one of the rare drugs that are not worth fucking with even once. Satisfy your opiate cravings with the occasional stray Vicodin.

CEASE USAGE IF: You dare to start.

A Note That Could Save Your or a Friend's Life

If you're with someone who is overdosing on anything—lost consciousness, stopped breathing, too hot or cold and clammy— CALL 911 IMMEDIATELY AND BEGIN ARTIFICIAL RESPIRATION. Many states and colleges have a Good Samaritan rule that protects people who call 911 to stop an overdose from prosecution for drug possession. (If you elect decent people, you get decent laws.) In those states and at those schools, by calling 911 for an overdosing friend, you are *not* risking prosecution. By not calling 911, you *are* risking death. If you're in doubt, call 911. It's the right thing to do.

A Final Word About Drugs

Just because lots of people experiment with drugs in college doesn't mean you have to. Should you choose to experiment with drugs—and booze is a drug, too—remember that honesty, integrity, and refusal to be pressured into doing stupid things will serve you well. Whatever you do, don't romanticize the drug habits of famous people like Miles Davis, Charles Bukowski, William Burroughs, Billie Holiday, Hunter S. Thompson, Ken Kesey, Lenny Bruce, Kurt Cobain, Ol' Dirty Bastard, or anybody else. You are not, and cannot be, them. You can only be you. As comedian (and recovering addict) Russell Brand pointed out when Amy Winehouse died: Some people have talent. Some people have the addiction disease. Some people have both. But, for the love of god, do not confuse one with the other.

9. A FEW WORDS ABOUT MANNERS

BY BETHANY JEAN CLEMENT AND LINDY WEST

A Few of the Basics

Don't talk with your mouth full. Use a coaster. If you want the ketchup, say, "Could you please pass the ketchup?" Then, when someone passes it to you, say, "Thank you!" When someone is talking to you, put down your goddamn phone and stop texting for one goddamn second. If someone sends you an invitation and asks you to RSVP, *RSVP*. If you go out to eat with people, bring cash. If someone asks you to do something but you're not interested but there's no way to decline without hurting their

feelings, say, "Yeah, I *might* take you up on that!" Then hide from that person forever. When you walk through a door, look behind you. If there is another person within 10 paces of you, hold the door for that person. If someone holds a door for you, say, "Thank you!" Be cordial to others, even if you are having a bad day (it's not their fault). Be a good loser and a gracious winner. Tip 20 percent. Don't be late. Listen.

How to Have a Conversation

Talking to people can be horrible (fuckin' people, all "LET'S TALK!!!"), but there are a few simple tricks that can make it easy. Nobody wants to hear about your dream. Nobody wants to hear about your dog. Nobody wants to hear about how you've noticed that some people say "soda" and other people say "pop." Instead, ask questions. Just ask questions. The only thing people love more than talking about themselves is LITERALLY NOTHING. With just a few choice words on your part, you can trick your conversational adversary into doing all the work. Words like "So, what do you do?" or "How long have you lived in [CITY]?" or "How about that danged sports team?" or "What was your relationship like with your dead mother?" Boom. Conversationed.

And hey, ladies—don't do that lady thing where you let yourself either fade into the background of a conversation or participate only as a sexual object. SAY STUFF. Look people in the eye, give a

firm handshake, speak up, and don't say yes if you really mean no. DON'T YOU DARE.

How to Take a Compliment

Brushing off a compliment not only is rude, it makes you look like an insecure basket case. If someone tells you that your hair looks nice, don't blush and look at the floor and mumble, "FUCK YOU! NO IT DOESN'T!" Instead, make eye contact and say, "Oh, thank you so much! That's so nice of you!" Smile and move on with your day with a spring in your step. Your hair looks nice! Good for you, Fonzie! You are not obligated to return the compliment, because that can come off as insincere. But if you really mean it, by all means throw one back.

How to Be a Guest at a Party

Bring something! Always bring something! (Unless it's a keg party. That is the only exception to the rule. The keg is all the party needs, and the keg will already be in attendance.) A bottle of wine is always welcome (or sparkling cider, if your friends are 13-year-old girls), or a nice wedge of cheese (or fake cheese, if your friends are mannequins). A six-pack (or more!) is completely acceptable. If you're close with the hosts and/or it's a small affair, call ahead and ask if there's anything they need. (Note: If you're a host and

you receive such a phone call, KEEP IT REASONABLE—no "Oh, could you just pick up some kimchi, eight small frozen chickens, and a jar of silver dragées?")

Most importantly, be gracious. If you go over to someone's house and they offer you a drink, *take it*. Don't poop all over their hospitality by being like, "Oh, no, thank you, I COULDN'T," over and over again, like that's some sort of altruistic gesture. Like you're the Gandhi of not-making-people-get-you-a-gin-and-tonic. These people are hosting you. Let them host. Don't make them beg. That said, don't get too drunk. Don't become the Gandhi of slurring "the proof is in the pudding" while groping for Melissa's pudding (vagina). Don't do that. Nobody wants that.

Smile! Chat (see How to Have a Conversation, page 140)! Talk to people you don't know. If you know the hosts well, offer to stay and help clean up (they'll probably say no, and you'll look good just for asking). Otherwise, leave before it starts to get weird. Don't be the last one there unless the host(s) have very specifically asked you to stay to help clean up or have sex.

How to Host a Party
. . . .

First, resign yourself to spending some money on your party. No, wait: CELEBRATE SPENDING SOME MONEY ON YOUR PARTY! YOUR PARTY'S GOING TO BE FACTUALLY THE BEST PARTY EVER! In order to have the best party ever, you will need bounty—bountiful snacks (they can be simple, just:

BOUNTY!), bountiful drinks, some napkins. You could deploy decorations, but why bother when you know the second secret to the best party ever, which is GOOD LIGHTING!? Good lighting is dim and makes people look like they should be kissed immediately. No one's going to be doing surgery at this party (um, right?)—kill the overheads. Get some candles (not scented—too stinky). Now, to populate your party universe: Invite humans! Invite those you really like—people who are capable of having conversations, people who are capable of drinking, people with mouths. Invite people from different parts of your life; they will enjoy to meet each other. Invite a few randoms, too—people you don't know especially well but who you've noticed have excellent shoes or a funny laugh or whatever. If these people ask whether they can bring anything, the only truly polite answer is "Oh, no! Of course not! Just come! Bring a friend!" If they are a truly polite person and/or have read this book, they will know to never, ever show up without bringing something.

Ding-dong! PARTY TIME! Wait, before this. Don't drink too much before your party starts, because (a) you want to enjoy this thoroughly, and (b) passing out at your own party is gauche and people might draw on your face. Okay, ding-dong! PARTY TIME! Welcome your guests heartily and give them a beverage! Keep your guests in beverages and snacks at pretty much all times—encourage them to help themselves, and sometimes say, "Do you need anything?" My, you are an awesome host. Also: Introduce the guests who don't know each other to each other, providing one hilarious fact (or fiction! Let

them sort it out!) about each person when you do the introducing. Don't let them huddle in cliques or stand alone facing walls. Maybe two people you introduce will get married someday! Maybe it'll be the first legal gay marriage on the moon and they'll thank you all across whatever the internet is then! Sweet.

The same basic rules apply to a dinner party, which is REALLY fun. Have one! (For some recipes, see What No One Else Will Tell You About Food, page 153.)

On Toilets

You're young, which means you're probably still all weird about pooping. That's okay—you'll get over it, and the sooner you do, the easier your life will be. Pooping is not that big a deal. If you have to poop in a department store, just go into the bathroom and do your poop. You can try to keep your poop quiet if you like, but don't sit there and sweat all day waiting for the bathroom to empty out, because that is both creepy (you are sitting there with your pants down listening to strangers pee!) and a waste of time. Just do it. Own your poop. Did you know that literally 100 percent of the other people in the department store bathroom have *also*, at one time or another, pooped? It's true! Probably that very day! If you have to poop at a party and there's only one bathroom, just do it. Flush as quickly as possible, light a match, turn on the fan, open a window, and walk out of that bathroom with your head held high. You have pooped with integrity. (Side note: If some of your poop

sticks to the side of the toilet bowl even after you've flushed, grab the toilet brush and scrub that shit off. It takes two seconds and it's the right thing to do. Don't leave it there like a tiny brown hostess gift.) Because here's the thing about pooping: NO ONE CARES. Not one person in the history of buttholes has ever turned to their friend and whispered, "Did you hear about Kevin? He *pooped*. IN THE BATHROOM. Tell everyone. Let's make sure he never has sex again." The only person thinking about your poop is you.

DO NOT PEE ON THE SEAT.

If you do, wipe it up.

If you use the last of the toilet paper, don't just get a new roll out of the cupboard and leave it on the floor next to the toilet. Actually *put it* on the thingy.

Ladies, as a general rule: Don't flush tampon applicators. They can really fuck up old plumbing. But don't put your used applicator all loosey-goosey in the trash can. Wrap it demurely in toilet paper. Nobody needs to see your womanly essence. (Also: Nobody needs to see plastic tampon applicators washed up on the beach, nor do we want them to be the main artifact left from our civilization after we are all extinct. Get the other kind, or the kind with no applicator, which are actually not gross.) (Also-also: Men, get over ladies' periods. Your body does things that are just as gross, and the ladies are very understanding about them.)

Most importantly, wash your hands. Wash your hands. Wash your hands. Wash your hands. Wash your hands. Wash your hands. Wash your hands. Wash your hands. Wash your hands. Wash your

hands. Wash your hands. Wash your hands. Wash your hands. Wash your hands. Wash your hands. Wash your hands. Wash your hands. Wash your hands. Wash your hands. Wash your hands. Wash your hands. Wash your hands. Wash your hands. Wash your hands. Wash your hands. Wash your hands. FOR GOD'S SAKE, WASH YOUR HANDS. NOBODY WANTS TO TOUCH YOUR PEE-HANDS.

Always knock.

10. HOW TO DO LAUNDRY

BY BETHANY JEAN CLEMENT

My father is congenitally incapable of doing laundry When I was a child, this deficit in his knowledge, in his complete understanding of all the things in the world and how each of them worked, was little short of shocking. He would try to do laundry, and he would fail, abjectly, a high percentage of the time. He knew, for example, to check each and every pocket of every clothing item before consigning it to the washing machine, and yet he consistently laundered ballpoint pens—consistently as in pretty much every time he did laundry. He always carried a pen (a grown-up thing), and a pen would find a way to sneak in. Safely inside the washing machine, inundated and churning around, the pen would work its way out of its pocket, divest itself of its cap, then

have its way with all the garments in the load—inking up stuff in a seemingly celebratory way, freed from the dull, controlled world of words into a glorious aqueous spree. That this would lead to the end of the pen—its lifeblood spilled and its shell consigned to the old bucket that acted as the basement trash can—concerned the pen not. While it lived, it truly lived. It ruined clothes.

My father, back before he was banned from doing laundry, also had a small but calamitous problem with sorting the light clothing from the dark. While segregation in general is to be very much avoided, in laundry it is a hallowed principle; it keeps your lighter clothes from slowly turning gray from the leaching dye of the darker clothes. My father could sort lights almost completely—his white dress shirts and T-shirts and underpants, mom's unmentionables and blouses, our smaller white socks and so forth—but, more often than seems believable, he would accidentally put in something bright red. It always seemed to be a T-shirt. Why did we have so many red T-shirts? The result: pink. Pink underwear, pink undershirts, pink everything in that load of laundry.

To be fair, my father is color-blind. This was a source of endless fascination to us when we were kids. Was the world like a black-and-white movie to Dad? How was, for example, the banananess of a banana compromised by such a deficit? What did he SEE? We were given to understand that it was a genetic thing, and that it only happened to men (the arbitrary mysteries of science). My brother was not color-blind, or so it seemed—but how could we, in truth, know how any other person saw anything? The mind reeled.

Meanwhile, there were many practical matters to be addressed. How did Dad know whether a traffic light was red or yellow or green? (Answer: The colors on a traffic light are always the same, top to bottom.) How could he get dressed without looking like a clown? (Answer: My mother arranged—she still does—the clothes hanging in his closet in sections according to what went with what, so he could dress in a kind of multiple-choice manner; same with the socks in his sock drawer. Somehow he still ends up with mismatched socks from time to time, and the sight of one of his ankles dark blue and the other brown fills me with a kind of tenderness I find difficult to describe.) We would badger him with tests: What color is this? What about this? Some weren't so much of a problem for him—orange, yellow—but still he always seemed like he was guessing, answering gamely but with a question mark at the end. With purples and maroons and forest greens and darker colors down to black, he was certainly guessing, and he often guessed wrong. It never occurred to us that this was a minor but real disability, and that he might not enjoy entertaining our questions about it; he was invincible, a superhero, even if he didn't know what color anything was.

Most bizarrely, my dad was unable to grasp the nature of bleach. Bleach was bleach; it said what it was, right in its name. My father, having sorted lights from darks, would splash in a healthy amount of bleach. With the dark clothes. He did this more than once. Having discovered his latest travesty of laundry, my mother would wail his name—Dan—mournfully from the basement: "DAAAAAAAaaaaaan!" Bleach removes color. If you add a little

bleach to a load of whites you're washing in hot water, it makes them whiter. If you put bleach on anything colored, it makes indelible spots of no-color-anymore. My father's difficulty with this basic principle was confounding. I asked him once about this: Why did he put bleach in with colors? "I thought it would brighten them up," he said sheepishly.

My father was barred from laundry, and when I was around 9 or 10, my parents contracted me to be the family's laundress. For this, I received the princely sum of $10 a week (which was more money back in the last century). I sorted lights from darks; I checked pockets (and got to keep any change or bills left behind); I used bleach on whites only; I folded clothes still warm from the dryer in the cool dim of the basement. (I got less afraid of the basement.) Dad's briefs were big enough to fold over into fourths. Mom's blouses and Dad's dress shirts went on hangers, hung on the edge of the ironing board. I laundered without incident, and with a small amount of pride.

Laundry has remained likable—and like most things, it's even more fun when you're not a kid anymore. In college, my roommate and I would have laundry parties: Along with the quarters and the detergent, you just need a jug of wine, which you drink to while away the laundry time. (We washed our whites together, and the pile of nice fresh socks commingling afterward was called the Sock Party, which is funnier when you've had some jug wine. Still: There's something funny, something sweet, about the clean socks of two friends in a pile.)

When my roommate went to France for a year, I did laundry with my goth friends Curtis and Elsa. They always seemed to have hash, and along with the washers and dryers in the dorm basement, there was a stove, so we'd do hot knives. It was weird and fun, just like Curtis and Elsa.

And in a situation where you have to go to a laundromat, you can get some good reading done and maybe make friends with the old guy who runs the laundromat and learn about all the potted plants he's got growing there. Or your laundromat might have the name Tiny Bubbles, which is something you can think about with a little glow of joy for the rest of your days: Tiny Bubbles.

How to Actually Do Laundry

WHAT YOU WILL NEED:

- Dirty clothes (machine washable—check the labels)
- Laundry detergent (powdered, in a box, means one less thing for the Great Pacific Garbage Patch)
- Bleach, maybe (See Note on page 152)
- Quarters, as required

Separate light-colored dirty clothes from dark ones. (Red counts as dark.) Launder lights and darks separately, unless you want all your clothes to converge on a uniform grayness.

Fire up the washer. Cold water is fine, in general, on normal cycle. Let the water start to fill the bottom of it, then sprinkle in your

laundry detergent. (You can use a little less than is recommended on the box. They want you to use more than you need, because: $.)

Add the clothes loosely. Do not cram. (Crammed-in clothes or an overfilled washer means nothing really gets clean.)

Close the lid. Enjoy a book or something to drink or both. (If you are at a laundromat or using other nonprivate machines, it's sad but true: You never know when someone might steal all your clothes. You probably want to stand by.)

You say the washer is done? Clean out the lint trap on the dryer (this prevents annoying fire and improves dryer performance). Put the clothes in the dryer. Make it go (medium temperature should be fine). Enjoy a book or something to drink or both.

Ding! That's it. For added niceness, fold while still warm, unless you're in Arizona or something.

A NOTE ABOUT BLEACH

Bleach is added, a quarter cup or so, along with the laundry detergent to the water in the washer before the clothes go in—white or very light clothes only. Use hot water for more whitening/brightening power, but be warned: Stuff that's new that's washed in hot water may shrink.

11. WHAT NO ONE ELSE WILL TELL YOU ABOUT FOOD

BY BETHANY JEAN CLEMENT AND CHRISTOPHER FRIZZELLE

How to (Not) Be a Foodie

S eriously, you do not want to be a "foodie." You do not want to even use the word "foodie," because it sounds so pretentious and stupid. And give up on finding a good substitute: There isn't one. Here's the thing: You are NOT a foodie—you are merely a person who has a modicum of knowledge about, and enjoys a variety

of, different foods. (This is very fashionable right now, and for good reason: It's healthier than a fast- and processed-food diet, and being willing to put almost anything in your mouth is hot.) Where should you begin? Eat food! Try all different kinds! Colleges and universities are places where cheap and interesting restaurants naturally congregate—there's a whole world of strange, delicious, inexpensive food out there. Look for places that are full and/or that have high ratings online, and go get some!

If you've never had dim sum (or even if you have), go with a bunch of friends. This is where you choose all kinds of crazy dumplings and noodley things and you-know-not-what from carts-on-wheels. The cart-wheeling ladies might be brusque, but don't be afraid to say yes to lots of stuff—it's all usually remarkably cheap, and the more you try, the more you'll like. (There may be chicken feet, which are actually kind of gross, but they're easy to avoid: They look like chicken feet.) Find a sushi place or a restaurant that serves oysters on the half shell (there's no law that says you have to order a full meal), and take a date. Taking someone to a place with interesting food makes you seem even greater than you already are, and eating raw seafood together is a bonding experience. (And if your date is adventurous about this, it bodes well for what else they might want to try.) Eat Indian food, Ethiopian, Latin American, pho, vegetarian, whatever—pizza's good, to be sure, but there's ALL THIS too. Find all-ages happy hours; it's a cheap way to eat at great places. Be ready with a wish list when someone else is paying or when you have some cash.

Always tip 20 percent when you eat in a restaurant, unless the server literally tells you to fuck off. Then you tip 10 percent. This is not a joke; servers work hard, and your tip is a large part of their pay—in some restaurants, it's all they get paid. Tip well or stay home.

If you start to get into it, you can read up on the foods of different cultures (Wikipedia is a fine start). Read some food writing—restaurant reviews in local papers and magazines, the dining section of the *New York Times* online, the food section of *The Stranger* online, food blogs, books by M. F. K. Fisher and John Thorne . . .

If you get super into it, you might find yourself reading cookbooks just for fun, whether you make a lot of stuff out of them or not—among the most awesome are Julia Child's *Mastering the Art of French Cooking* and anything by Marcella Hazan.

Marcella Hazan's prose, embedded right in her cookbooks, is like your bossy but amazing and funny grandma—she knows everything about Italian food and wants you to DO IT RIGHT (and she also smokes tons of Marlboro Lights and drinks lots of whiskey).

Julia Child was a very tall woman with a warbling voice who devoted years of her life to making a French cookbook for Americans—you also HAVE to read her memoir, *My Life in France*, and watch some of her old cooking shows on YouTube (if you can find the one where she drops a duck on the floor while trying to prepare it, you will learn that being uptight is just not where cooking's at—she pretty much invented the five-second

rule). Oh! And you have to watch the parts of the movie *Julie &*
Julia with Meryl Streep. In order to play Julia Child, Streep ate
Kermit the Frog: The voice—the chortle-yodeling, the vowels—is
perfect. Streep's physical embodiment of Child is perfect, too, both
graceful and ungainly (Child towered, thick through the middle,
over almost everyone). The moments in which Streep-as-Child
masters the art of French cooking at Le Cordon Bleu are comedy
nonpareil. And Streep-as-Child is sexy: When she looks down into
Stanley Tucci's eyes and pulls down his suspenders in a scene that
stops just before their daily Paris nooner: hel-LO. (Tucci, as short,
shiny-domed, bespectacled Paul Child, is weirdly, completely hot.)
Every scene with Streep in it is endlessly engrossing. She opens an
envelope on a porch, glancing slightly wildly over her shoulder, and
it is magic. (But you should fast-forward through the Julie parts of
Julie & Julia, because they are pretty terrible.)

Anyhow! Go to the farmers' market, browse, talk to people.
Learn to cook some simple, tasty things—it really is easy, don't be
afraid! (See the following recipes and get a good, simple cookbook
to start—the ones from *Cook's Illustrated* are neat.) Maybe learn
a little about wine (see Wine, What the Hell's the Deal?, page 124).
In general, with food—as with all things—do not bloviate. Rather,
share your secrets. Be excited. Bring a date, or make some food for
one. They will love you.

So You're a Vegetarian!

Good for you! Don't be an asshat about it. It's easy: Don't preach, and if you get invited to eat food, let your host know, but tell them you don't need any special treatment (then don't need any special treatment).

A Really Easy, Really Pretty, Really Good Soup You Can Make With a Butternut Squash

Butternut squash is a hilarious-looking vegetable with fucking delicious insides. Find the biggest one at the grocery store, all beige and giant-peanut-like.

Then take it home and cut it in half. Each half will have a little bowl of cute seeds in it; scrape out these seeds. Then drizzle olive oil on the orangey insides, set both halves in a pan filled with a half inch of water, and put the pan in the oven at 400 degrees F for 45 minutes. While the oven softens up the squash, dice up a huge onion and toss it, along with some butter, in a stockpot, with lots of salt and pepper, and cook it (stirring some) over medium heat until the onion is soft. When you take the squash out of the oven after 45 minutes, it'll be all hot and mad, but pretty soft and nice-smelling. Take a spoon and scoop all the squash out of its skin and put it in the stockpot with the onions, and then pour a container of organic chicken broth over it (regular chicken broth is fine, too). Then just let it bubble on low heat for a while. Bubble, bubble, bubble.

After a while bubbling in that chicken broth, the squash will get really soft. The orangey hunks become a chunky puree. Put in some more pepper, and a little cinnamon, and if you have any, some nutmeg and fresh herbs. Try it with a spoon. Goddamn! Good, huh? You can eat it like this if you want—a very chunky butternut squash soup—but you might as well go all the way and fancy it up by putting it in a blender and blending it. You might have to do it in batches. If you don't have a ladle to get the chunky soup into the blender, use a coffee mug. Once all of it has been blended into golden smoothness, pour some into a bowl, put a plop of organic sour cream in the middle, and eat it.

With any luck, it'll be raining outside. Eating butternut squash soup while it's raining is the best.

How to Make Tacos

If you're a know-nothing, talentless bore, you can just go to the store and get one of those packets of taco seasoning and add it to any meat you like. But who wants to be a know-nothing, talentless bore? Don't you want to have a "specialty"? Don't you want to impress you-know-who? If so, make this your specialty: spicy shredded chicken tacos from scratch. You-know-who will *definitely* want to make love to you after you've made spicy shredded chicken tacos from scratch.

Here's what you do: Go to the store and buy some boneless, skinless chicken. Also buy a large onion, one or two containers of

chicken broth, chili powder (note: don't confuse chili powder with chili flakes), tortillas, and whatever other taco fixings you like—salsa and/or fresh tomato, avocado, cheese, sour cream (a must—organic tastes way better!), black beans (for maximum goodness, fancy 'em up with cumin, also found in the spice aisle), and cilantro.

When you get home, put the chicken in a large pot and add the chicken broth, enough to cover however much chicken you've bought. You are going to very slowly simmer that chicken in that chicken broth until those breasts fall apart on their own. This takes some time—about three hours (and if three hours have gone by without noticeable falling-apart, pull apart the chicken with two forks). While three hours of slow cooking sounds like a pain, imagine how nice and warm and chicken-y your place is going to smell by the time you're done. Keep the heat on the low end of medium, and put a lid on the pot, with a little breathing room for steam to come out.

But wait! Right away, chop up a large onion and add it to the simmering pot—the onion plus the broth are going to do the bulk of the work, flavorwise. Then add salt, pepper (freshly cracked, if possible), and chili powder. The amount of chili powder is directly related to how spicy it will be, so just use a little at first, and later, when the broth has mostly boiled away, leaving delicious, falling-apart chicken, you can dip a fork in, taste the chicken, and add more chili powder to your liking.

Final tip for maximum greatness in your mouth: Heat the tortillas in a skillet covered in salt.

How to Make Very Tasty Pasta

There are so many ways! The most basic, a.k.a. Emergency Pasta, goes like this: Put a big pot of water on the stove on high, and put a handful of salt in the water. (Truly, a handful: Don't be shy! Unless you have extra-giant hands.) Choose your favorite pasta shape of the moment (the brand Barilla costs a little bit more, but it's worth it). When the water boils, put the pasta in and wiggle it all around with a big spoon so that none of it sticks together. Then grate some decent-quality Parmesan or, really, whatever cheese you happen to have around. If you have some pine nuts or other unsalted nuts, toast them (without any oil) in a pan on the stove on medium (watch carefully, they like to burn!). If you have some tomato, dice it up. Cook the pasta for the lesser amount of time on the box, then dip a piece out and taste it; repeat every minute or so until it's the way you like it. Drain it and toss it in a bowl (or top it on a plate) with a good drizzling of olive oil, the cheese, the nuts, the tomatoes, and some fresh herbs if you have any (or dried if not—smell 'em and find one you like), plus lots of salt and pepper. Voilà! (A tip: If you're serving it to a date, don't call it Emergency Pasta.)

Sauce is almost as easy. You'll need: an onion, garlic, olive oil, salt and pepper, a big can of plum tomatoes, half a little can of tomato paste (optional), and some dried or fresh oregano and/or basil. Dice up the onion into pieces about an inch big, smash/de-skin a few cloves of garlic, and put it all in a skillet with a good splash of olive oil on medium heat. Salt and pepper it well. Cook until the

onion is golden-translucent and floppy. (If you like meat, you can cut up some sausage or crumble some ground beef, and cook it with the onion.) Pour in the plum tomatoes (and the tomato paste if you want), and kind of chop/mangle up the big pieces. Add a spoonful of dried oregano/basil if you've got 'em; if you have fresh, wait until before you serve. Now it can simmer on low heat for anywhere from 10 minutes to an hour—it doesn't really matter, though it gets more reduced and richer with time. Cook your pasta as in the paragraph above, and serve it with lots of grated Parmesan (not from a green can). Voilà!

How to Make the World's Best Macaroni and Cheese (With a Monogram on It!)

This recipe takes some time, but it is completely worth it. Get all your ingredients out and ready (professionals call it, Frenchily, *mise en place*, or "everything in place") before you start. Consider smoking some marijuana first, if you're into that and won't lose track of what the hell you're doing.

1 pound large elbow macaroni (penne if you're feeling fancy)

5 tablespoons butter

¼ cup all-purpose flour

2½ cups organic whole milk

About 5 ounces cheddar, sliced: sharp is good, as is Irish cheddar*

About 4 ounces Gruyère, sliced

About 2 ounces Parmesan, sliced

Pinch of ground nutmeg

Dash of Tabasco or Tapatio

Salt and freshly ground black pepper

About 4 ounces mozzarella, cut into ¼-inch cubes

About 2 ounces Parmesan, grated

Paprika

Bread crumbs, preferably homemade, but whatever

A couple slices of better-quality presliced white bread

Melted butter, for brushing bread

You can use pretty much any cheeses for this recipe, just the same overall amount. Organic is better; organic Monterey Jack sounds boring but is delicious (and could be used in place of the mozzarella). Parmigiano-Reggiano is nice, but really, this is just mac and cheese, people.

Preheat oven to 350 degrees F. Lightly butter a rectangular baking dish (you might have enough for a little round casserole dish, too).

Cook the pasta until just al dente (that is, not quite all the way done). Drain and rinse with cold water.

Get yourself a beverage. The roux/whisking-in-cheese takes a while and can get hot.

Melt the butter in a large/deep skillet or saucepan over medium heat. Whisk in flour and cook, stirring constantly, for one minute.

(Look, you made a roux!)

Slowly whisk in milk, then cook for one to two minutes, or until lightly thickened to the consistency of cream.

Drop in the slices of cheddar, Gruyère, and Parm one or two at a time, whisking constantly, letting them mostly melt before adding more. Season with nutmeg, a dash of hot sauce, and salt and pepper. Remove from heat.

In a large bowl, combine cheese sauce and pasta. Stir in the mozzarella. Transfer to the prepared baking dish. Sprinkle with grated Parm, paprika to your liking, and bread crumbs ditto.

Cut pertinent initials or symbols out of slices of white bread with a sharp knife. Position artfully on top of macaroni, then brush liberally with melted butter.

Bake until the cheese is bubbling and the top is browned, 25 to 35 minutes.

Makes eight-ish servings. Hi!

How to Make an Impressive Entire Roasted Chicken

This is way easier than you'd think, but tongs are VERY helpful for the part where you turn the chicken. (This recipe is adapted from *Cook's Illustrated*'s *The Best Recipe*—*Cook's Illustrated* does things like roast 209 chickens in 209 different ways to find the very best method. Their cookbooks also have neat essays about all their experiments, the science behind cooking, different kinds of pans, and stuff like

that.) Paying a couple dollars more for a free-range, or natural, or organic chicken is worth it (Trader Joe's has a good selection). Maybe make this one for your roommates before you try it on a date.

Julia Child suggests that you serve roasted chicken with "a light red wine, such as a Bordeaux-Médoc, or a rosé." Fancy! (See Wine: What the Hell's the Deal?, page 124.)

> 8 or so of those small red potatoes (or fancy small red/gold/purple mix)
>
> Olive oil
>
> Salt and pepper
>
> 3- to 5-pound whole chicken
>
> Butter

Heat oven to 375 degrees F (move the rack to the middle). Cut the potatoes in half and put them in a rectangular baking dish with a good splash of olive oil; salt and pepper liberally; and stir them around to get them a little oily. (You can add mushrooms, carrots, turnips, and dried or fresh rosemary or other herbs, too.) Take the giblets—they're those weird things inside the chicken—out of the inside of the chicken, and put them in among the potatoes. Rinse the chicken, inside and out, and pat it lovingly dry with a paper towel or two. Set it on top of the potatoes, one wing up. Important: To avoid potentially horrible illness, wash your hands and any surface the raw chicken has touched with hot, soapy water. Put a pat or two of butter on the chicken, and salt and pepper it liberally.

Roast your bird (that just means put it in the oven and bake it) wing-side-up for 15 minutes. Pull it out, turn it other-wing-side-up,

pat-of-butter and salt/pepper it, and roast it for another 15 minutes. Pull it out, turn it breast-up (with the drumsticks sticking up in the air), pat-of-butter and salt/pepper it, turn the oven up to 450 degrees F, and put it back in for approximately half an hour.

Check it! You will know it is done when the drumstick wiggles in the socket readily and/or when juices run clear yellow when you stab it. (It doesn't hurt to stab pretty deep in and look for any pinkness, meaning it's not done, until you've made enough chickens that you have a good sense of doneness.) Cut it up and serve it with the delicious potatoes from underneath. And try the different giblets; some people like them.

Make Your Own Coffee!

You will save lots of money (and probably make new friends) if you make your own coffee. Get a coffeemaker or a French press or whatever, and get some decent-quality coffee (Trader Joe's beans are pretty good and relatively cheap, and they have a grinder), and free yourself from the bonds of the evil mermaid! She only likes you for your cash.

Organic Food: WTF?

Everyone's all, "Organic, *organic*, ORGANIC!" these days, and there are some pretty damn convincing political and environmental and health reasons. But it also makes sense to eat local (smaller

carbon footprint) and seasonal (fresher, nicer) food, like from a farmers' market, and it's hard for little farmers to get certified organic because the USDA is big and mean. (You want to know more? Read all about it on our friend the internet!) Organic is also often markedly more expensive. Some things that reportedly have more pesticides—and thus are better to buy organic—include lettuce, spinach, bell peppers, celery, potatoes, apples, peaches, nectarines, strawberries, pears, and cherries. Organic milk and cheese tend to taste a lot better than their nonorganic counterparts. And meat can have some pretty weird stuff done to it if it comes from a factory farm; eat less meat, and you can spend a little more to get the good stuff. But you know what? If you're cooking real food—instead of eating processed food or junk food or fast food or sweets, or existing on soda pop—you're doing good. Don't worry too much about the rest of it.

12. WHAT NO ONE ELSE WILL TELL YOU ABOUT MUSIC, BOOKS, AND ART

BY GRANT BRISSEY, PAUL CONSTANT, CHRISTOPHER FRIZZELLE, ERIC GRANDY, JEN GRAVES, AND DAVID SCHMADER

How to Be Into Music Without Annoying Everyone

U nless you're already a sanctioned record nerd, or well on your way, you may find yourself entrapped by some predictable progressions upon entering college. Some of

the most common (boring) phases are: the Pink Floyd Phase, the Bob Dylan Phase, the Jimi Hendrix Phase (if it didn't take in high school), or, god forbid, the Bob Marley Phase (resist the temptation to grow dreadlocks, especially if you are white). If you do experience symptoms of such a phase, embrace it but keep it brief, and don't make a big deal about it—no posters on the wall, no talking people's ear off.

As a rule, music talk should generally be avoided, unless you're saying something to the effect of "Have you heard them/him/her/it?" or "Yes! I love them/him/her/it. Put it on!" or "No, I've never heard them/him/her/it. Let's hear it!" or "No, they/he/she/it have/has never really done it for me." Always admit when you don't know an artist, record, or song; anyone who would judge you for not knowing is not worth your time, and it's often easily exposed when you lie about things in such uncharted territory. Plus, you'll never learn it if you pretend to already know it. If you must jibber-jabber about music for any length of time, watch it with the genre names, bub. Half the time they mean something different to everyone involved, and using them just makes you sound like an asshole music critic, and no one wants to hang out with those dudes.

Once you have expediently processed your Bob Dylan Phase, investigate his superior alternative Leonard Cohen, starting with *Songs from a Room* and ending long before the second half of his discography. Pink Floyd? Chuck everything but *The Piper at the Gates of Dawn*. Hendrix? You can go wherever you like after Jimi, but keep all of his records because he is a god. Marley? Put the bong

away (or in the trash if it features a skull and/or jester likeness) and get yourself in touch with Desmond Dekker, who traded more in rocksteady, which you should be listening to instead of reggae anyway—it precedes Marley, it's slower, and it's better. Also, get onto some classic dub records—King Tubby's *At the Controls* is an excellent start.

What the Albums in Your Dorm Room Say About You

THE BEATLES: You own an album. **THE ROLLING STONES**: You own two albums. **THE BEACH BOYS**: You have never surfed in your life. **THE CLASH**: You're experimenting with Marxism. **SLEATER-KINNEY**: You're experimenting with lesbianism. **BELLE & SEBASTIAN**: You're experimenting with acting gay to get the girls who are experimenting with lesbianism. **MINOR THREAT**: You're straight-edge and no fun at parties. **FUGAZI**: Used to be straight-edge, still no fun at parties. **Q AND NOT U**: Used to be straight-edge, learned how to dance, finally fun at parties! **JAWBREAKER**: You get sentimental about punk shows. **LCD SOUNDSYSTEM**: You get sentimental about dance parties. **PHISH**: You were in high school jazz band, and now you smoke pot. **BOB MARLEY**: Your parents know you smoke pot. **THE RAMONES/SEX PISTOLS**: You resent your parents for paying your tuition. **PUBLIC IMAGE LTD.**: You're in communications. **ARCADE FIRE**: You're in musical theater. **DEVO**: You're in experimental arts. **VAMPIRE WEEKEND**: You wish you'd gotten into a better school.

PAVEMENT: You test well but don't do your homework. **PUBLIC ENEMY**: You resent "the Man" and/or are embarrassed about being the offspring of "the Man." **THE NOTORIOUS B.I.G.**: You're a chubby-chaser with necrophilia. **LIL WAYNE**: You love comedy and possibly cough syrup. (No homo!) **LADY GAGA**: You hate social injustice and possibly pants. (Yes homo!) **PRINCE**: You are funky, sexually freaky. **AL GREEN**: You are tastefully horny and likely to be a good lover. **TOBY KEITH**: Your dick smells like goat butt. **GLEE SOUNDTRACK**: You hate music.

What the Art Posters in Your Dorm Room Say About You

You think that a Salvador Dalí poster says that you are arty and take interesting drugs. But it does not; it says that you think a melting clock painted in 1930 is still avant-garde. You must take this down. A Mondrian poster is probably best if you go modern, but sharper would be a poster of a work of modern architecture. (Remember, modern is not the same as contemporary.) The color fields of Rothko are a cliché, but still workable for the sensitive (Rothko's paintings elicit more crying than any other modern artist's). If you must have one, try to say something cool about it, like, "Did you know that Rothko wanted his paintings to fill your entire field of vision, so that's how far you should stand from them?" It's true; situate your bed accordingly and you've got yourself a pickup line.

Everything You Need to Know to Successfully Flirt With a Film Ner

THE BIRTH OF A NATION *(1915)*: D. W. Griffith's silent epic about the inherent superiority of the white man, set before and during the American Civil War. It's the highest-grossing film of the silent era, the first film to cut between two scenes, and so boring you will die. **CITIZEN KANE** *(1941)*: After a tumultuous career, a mentally ill newspaper mogul dies alone and friendless. Celebrated for its unprecedentedly intricate cinematic storytelling and writer/director/star Orson Welles' astonishingly successful display of artistic hubris. Rosebud is a sled. **THE SEARCHERS** *(1956)*: Hailed as the greatest western ever made, John Ford's *The Searchers* stars John Wayne as a laconic loner on the hunt for a girl kidnapped by evil Native Americans. In one hilarious scene, a dim-witted cowpoke kicks a sleeping Indian squaw, who rolls down a rocky hill, breaking many bones. **THE MALTESE FALCON** *(1941)*, **DOUBLE INDEMNITY** *(1944)*, **THE THIRD MAN** *(1949)*, **SUNSET BLVD.** **(1950)**, **THE BIG HEAT** *(1953)*, and **TOUCH OF EVIL** *(1958)*: These are all "film noir," a genre of stylish crime films filled with cynical men, deadly dames, and long shadows. "Noir" rhymes with "Gwar." **2001: A SPACE ODYSSEY** *(1968)*: A gorgeous film about the world's boringest space adventure, with long, slow, extended segments devoid of dialogue. Noted for its extravagant pre-CGI visual effects and early acknowledgement of the evilness of computers.

THE GODFATHER *(1972)*: Francis Ford Coppola's deeply perfect mob drama chronicles the transfer of power from the elderly Don Corleone (a middle-aged Marlon Brando) to his son Michael (a young Al Pacino). The pristine first installment was followed by 1974's imperfect but awesome *The Godfather: Part II* and 1990's ridiculous *The Godfather: Part III*. **A WOMAN UNDER THE INFLUENCE** *(1974)*: Writer/director/sadist John Cassavetes' most rewarding cinematic torture session, starring the heroic Gena Rowlands as a lady who goes totally fucking crazy in all sorts of shocking, dull, and disturbing ways, for a long, long time. **NATIONAL LAMPOON'S ANIMAL HOUSE** *(1978)*: A chilling documentary about the dark side of college life, from binge drinking to statutory rape. Watch and learn.

Spoiler Alerts for the Big Novels So You Can Flirt With English Nerds as If You've Already Read Them

MOBY-DICK: Everyone dies except the whale and Ishmael, who floats to safety while clinging to Queequeg's coffin. What you should say: "Everyone skips over the chapter about different classifications of whales, but it's actually one of the funniest parts—a parody of encyclopedic writing and, if you think about it, knowledge itself." **INVISIBLE MAN**: After finding momentary glory as a political activist, the narrator is mistaken for a sellout named Rhinehart and is forced into a dark basement by angry

men. While it appears he's lost everything, he believes that his story—this novel—is his political legacy. What you should say (if you're not black): "I never dreamed that I could get so close to the African-American experience." If you are black, just stare sullenly out the window without saying a word. **THREE LIVES**: Gertrude Stein's first published book is made up of three novellas: "The Good Anna" ends with Anna dying of working too hard. At the end of "Melanctha," Melanctha dies of consumption after contemplating suicide. "The Gentle Lena" closes with Lena dying during the birth of her fourth child, who does not survive. What you should say (while shaking your head): "It's just so . . . raw." **ULYSSES:** After a long day on the town, Leopold Bloom returns home, pees in his backyard, and goes to bed. As he falls asleep, his wife, Molly, reflects on the time they got engaged. What you should say: *"Ulysses* isn't nearly as challenging as everyone says—it just requires a serious reader, is all." **MRS. DALLOWAY**: She has a party where she hears about mentally ill veteran Septimus Warren Smith's suicide and she reflects on the kindness he showed her. What you should say: "The clever similarities to *Ulysses* really make this a riposte from Woolf to Joyce about women's roles in society." **THE GREAT GATSBY**: A man whose wife has been fucking around on him mistakenly shoots Gatsby to death in his swimming pool, and even though tons of assholes used to come to Gatsby's parties, no one goes to his funeral. What you should say: "The parallels to our own time are stunning."

Books You Should Avoid

While you're in college, you should avoid Ayn Rand. Seriously, you'll thank us later. Sometimes, college students—especially white college students from middle-class-or-higher backgrounds—read her humorless but weirdly compelling novels and start to think that they've somehow pulled themselves up by their own bootstraps. They then become annoying pricks for approximately eight years, at least. Don't read Salman Rushdie's *The Satanic Verses*. The first half is mostly about how you should have a good time without hurting anyone else, which is fine. The second half is pseudomystical mumbo jumbo that has convinced a good number of acid casualties that they're Wiccan high priests. Rushdie is talented, but skip this one. Ladies, if your grandmother sends you a book by SARK, put it down and back away—otherwise, one day you might wake up a 67-year-old cat lady with cornrows and turquoise paint in between your toes. (Same with Rhonda Byrne's *The Secret*.) Skip Charles Bukowski right now, too—Bukowski will convince you that chronic assholism is a lifestyle, when it's just a hobby. And remember: *Fight Club* is a satire, not a lifestyle choice.

13. WHAT NO ONE ELSE WILL TELL YOU ABOUT POLITICS

BY BETHANY JEAN CLEMENT, CHRISTOPHER FRIZZELLE, GOLDY, DAVID SCHMADER, AND LINDY WEST

Getting Started

So you wanna make a difference, huh? You're young, you're strong, you're entering your intellectual prime, and you're just itching to stand up to the arrogant gray-hairs of your parents' generation—who, admittedly, royally screwed things up—and set our nation right again. You want to end injustice,

175

end poverty, end pollution, end wars, and push the powers that be toward smarter, fairer, and more sustainable policies. In other words, like generations of politically conscious students before you, you want to change the world.

Well, here's a novel idea: *You could fucking vote!*

Yeah, sure, marches and rallies and sit-ins are great and all that, but if you really want to make a difference—if you really want to strike fear into the sclerotic hearts of the political establishment and force reforms that make a difference in the here and now—you and all your classmates will register the fuck to vote and then go goddamn vote!

Honestly . . . how hard is it? It's like an open-book quiz you've had months to prepare for, and it's multiple fucking choice! And yet most young people don't vote. Lift up your eyes and look around the library or lecture hall in which you're reading this: On average, four out of five of your fellow schoolmates didn't bother to vote.

Now look at yourself. Did you vote? No? *Asshole.*

And don't say that voting doesn't matter, or that your one vote out of millions can't possibly make a difference, because it does and it can. Those annual tuition hikes you and your parents are forced to swallow (and yes, more are on the way) come from a government that doesn't fear you, a government that's more concerned with the whiny don't-raise-my-taxes concerns of home-owning oldsters who actually vote than with the generation of I'm-too-cool-to-vote kiddies like you, who current homeowners are counting on to change their bedpans and give them minimum-wage sponge baths a

few years down the road. Oh sure, politicians love to talk about how you're the future, but they're up for reelection and people your age don't vote, so who the fuck do you think they're going to pander to?

So yeah, march and protest and rally all you want. Join your student government, volunteer for your favorite candidates, all that's great. Do it. But above all, if you really want to help fix our nation's broken political system—if you really want to change the world—vote, goddamn it! Or shut the fuck up.

How to Know If You're a Republican or a Democrat

Sweeping generalizations are never a good idea—but here we go! Republicans believe that money is the most important thing. For example, if a corporation wants to make a bunch of money in a manner that has the unfortunate side effect of spewing fluorescent orange goo into the air, Republicans will be all, "Fluorescent orange goo is perfectly safe and kinda tasty!" because goo-spewing is good for business, and good business means good jobs, and good jobs means more money. Democrats believe other things—like equal rights and the sustainability of the planet—are as important, if not more important, than making as much money as possible, so they're more inclined to be all, "Um, can we limit the amount of fluorescent orange goo here, please?" Because of this, Republicans laugh about how Democrats are tree-huggers and owl-kissers and socialists and hippies. Meanwhile, Democrats

laugh about how Republicans are well-fed, oil-covered, cigar-smoking pieces of shit.

Republicans also believe that Jesus is the most important thing, or at least lately they pretend to in order to win elections. They furrow their brows and pretend like gay marriage is the worst horror that could ever befall society, for example, even though Jesus said nothing about gay marriage or gay people. Pro-life Republicans invoke "Thou shalt not kill" in all seriousness when it comes to a clump of cells that will eventually become a baby, but they have no problem killing an actual adult human who's on death row (even though there are many instances of wrongful convictions in the history of death row). Nor do they have a problem with war—after all, war is a big business—even though wars tend to result in deaths.

Republicans fully believe the unregulated free market will sort everything out, even when it comes to Wall Street and health care, which is insane, because an unregulated Wall Street caused the Great Recession and unregulated health care means corporations make all the rules. Republicans tend to favor tax cuts for the very rich, insisting that the rich are "job creators," even though they're constantly creating jobs overseas, where it's cheaper; Democrats tend to favor tax cuts for the middle class, because if you give the middle class more of their own money back they will *spend* it, which helps the economy. On social issues, Republicans characterize Democrats as pot-smoking, public-transportation-riding, casual-sex-having moral relativists, and even though that does describe 86 percent of the staff of *The Stranger*, that's just as unfair of a generalization of

Democrats as all the negative generalizations about Republicans we just discussed.

The truth is, politics is a shifting, sliding thing, defined in large part by political leaders, who change all the time. Republicans will tell you with glee that Abraham Lincoln was a Republican, even though the Republican Party of today has nothing to do with the Republican Party of the 1860s. Be engaged, ask questions, get your information from sources other than TV or your parents, and you'll figure out where you fall on the spectrum soon enough. (Hint: Don't be a Republican. They're morons at best, fucking evil at worst.)

Take It Easy on Tattooing Yourself in Your Beliefs

Never forget that you are still a freakishly pliable, under-construction human being—that's why it's great you're in college!—and you should do your best to refrain from ascribing permanence to your gloriously fleeting feelings (i.e., no tattoos of "BI AND PROUD!," "Communist and Lovin' It!," or the lyrics to some stupid song you may love now but will resent the shit out of in 10 years).

When It's Okay to Yell at Someone About Politics

Let's say you're at a party, and that it's a party for Christians, put on by a Christian video game company, and Jesus Christ himself is

there. (TRUE STORY! How do you get yourself into these things? Answer: free drinks.) Jesus is wearing a long white toga-type thing and a special Jesus sash, and he has lustrous long hair—not like dirty-unkempt-hippie-guy hair, but beautiful, shiny, wavy brown hair. It cannot be denied: Jesus is hot. "JESUS CHRIST!" you say. "Yes!" he beams. "So, wait: Are you really Jesus?" you say, testing the waters. "Like, do the people here, and/or you yourself, believe that you are Jesus? Or are you just a guy hired to be dressed up as Jesus?" And Jesus leans in and says, "Totally the latter. I don't even believe in God!" So then you talk to Jesus while you finish your drink, and then you dance with Jesus for a while. Jesus is such a good dancer. You get your picture taken with him by the professional-photographer-guy, because: It's Jesus!

You're swept up in the magic of the nearness of Jesus and free drinks, so you say to the professional-photographer-guy who's taking your photo with Jesus, "So, are *you* Christian? Or were you just hired to take pictures here?" You're thinking you and Jesus might have a new friend. But no! Professional-photographer-guy is a believer. He conveys this in a humble yet still somehow self-satisfied manner. Again, you've had a few drinks. "But what about the gays?" you say. "I believe Jesus loves and accepts everyone," Christian-professional-photographer-guy says. "So, then, you support gay rights, like gay marriage?" you say. "Oh, I'm really not educated about it enough to have an opinion," he says with vacant sincerity. "What the hell does that mean?" you say. "Denying gay people their rights is a political platform of your entire religious

institution—the institution that you've entrusted your soul to," you say. He says again that he believes Jesus loves and accepts everyone. You say again that it's his moral responsibility to develop a point of view about one of the current political tenets of his faith. "Oh," Christian-professional-photographer-guy says. "I just really haven't given it much thought." "MAYBE YOU SHOULD GIVE IT SOME MOTHERFUCKING THOUGHT," you suggest. You're rarely so combative, but his ignorance—real or feigned—makes you incensed.

Christian-professional-photographer-guy remains empty-eyed as he offers more empty words. You're cursing freely; you're close to berating him. You realize there's no point. "There's no point to this," you say. Christian-professional-photographer-guy touches you lightly on the forearm and tells you he's glad you talked and that he's really going to think about it. "LIKE HELL YOU'RE GOING TO THINK ABOUT IT! IF YOU WERE CAPABLE OF CRITICAL THINKING WE WOULDN'T BE HAVING THIS CONVERSATION!" you shout. "FUCKING FUCK!" you shout, and you reel away. You will still be mad when you wake up the next day.

The moral of the story is this: It's often pointless to talk to people about politics, and in general it's very rude to shout at people at parties, but sometimes you've got to do what you've got to do.

What No One Else Will Tell You About Feminism

··

GUESS WHAT? YOU ARE A FEMINIST.

If you are a person alive in the world, other people, both men and women, have told you that all feminists are hairy, reactionary, undersexed, man-hating bitches who need to quit cryin' (because we have suffrage now! And Roombas!). HOWEVER. THAT IS OBVIOUSLY STUPID. Feminism is not a radical movement or a fringe movement or an embarrassment or a fraud. Feminism is simple. The "patriarchy" does "exist." To identify as a feminist is to acknowledge that women are people, and, as such, women deserve the same social, economic, and political rights and opportunities as other styles of people (i.e., men-people). To be a feminist is also to acknowledge that the world is not, currently, a fair and just and safe place for women to exist. Because it is not. Obviously (see: everything ever). To deny these things makes you, at worst, a bad person who hates women, including but not limited to: Sarah Michelle Gellar, Jennifer Garner, Jennifer Aniston, Jennifer Lopez, your mother, Jennifer Lopez's mother, Jennifer Garner's Aunt Marcy, Michelle Obama, Ellen DeGeneres, Cher, Julie Andrews, Kim Kardashian, Khloe Kardashian, Kourtney Kardashian, Kraken Kardashian, Karphone Kardashian, Kickball Kardashian, Kornkob Kardashian, and THE VIRGIN FUCKING MARY. At best, it makes you a complacent idiot.

ONE MORE TIME: If you are not a feminist (or something blamelessly ignorant, like a baby or a ferret or a college freshman), then you are a bad person. Those are the only options. You either believe that women are people, or you don't. To help you pick one, here is some information!

FIRST-WAVE FEMINISM: MAYBE WE COULD BE CITIZENS NOW?

These were the tough old 19th-century bitchez (note: Calling women "bitchez" with an affectionate *z* is pretty upper-level ironic material—maybe just stick with "women" for now) like Susan B. Anthony and Elizabeth Cady Stanton who were all, "Heeeeccy bros, we were thinking that maybe if you're not busy we could get the right to vote and stuff please maybe?" Then they proceeded to righteously fuck shit up until the ratification of the 19th amendment in 1920, which gave American women the vote. A lot of the first-wavers were totally racist, plus they were still pretty into the idea that a woman's job is shutting up and scrubbing stuff. But, you know, nobody's perfect.

SECOND-WAVE FEMINISM: MAYBE YOU COULD STOP RAPING US, PLEASE?

After World War II, women started to be like, "Oh! Maybe I can get a job and tell my husband to stop raping me!" They began taking on subtler forms of sexism and misogyny—things that might not be legally mandated (like voting rights) but were fucking up women's

lives nonetheless. These women would become the second-wavers. In 1963, Betty Friedan made everyone go crazy by suggesting that the nuclear family might be a crock of shit that stifled women's potential and made them unhappy. Then sooooooo many things happened!!! Birth control pills, illegalization of marital rape (in all states, FINALLY, in 1993!), *Griswold v. Connecticut*, affirmative action rights for women, Title IX, *Roe v. Wade*, and SO MUCH MORE—look it up on Wikipedia, seriously. (Fun fact: Bras were not actually burned.) There was much arguing about pornography (zzzzzz). The Equal Rights Amendment did not pass. Once shit started to get done, shrewd anti-feminists took the opportunity to declare sexism officially over, because women were now allowed to not be raped (sometimes) and also to work for low wages in garment factories and rapey advertising agencies, and therefore any woman who complained about anything from this moment onward was a hairy, braless bitch. Women continued to fight, because women are awesome. Fuck Phyllis Schlafly.

THIRD-WAVE FEMINISM: MAYBE I LIKE RAPE! SHUT UP! MAYBE I DON'T! SHUT UP!

One day, someone had the gall to point out that the term "women" encompasses more than just "upper-middle-class disgruntled white housewives." Immigrant women exist. Trans-women exist. Entirely *gruntled* upper-middle-class white housewives exist. Sex workers exist. Third-wave feminism is the idea that women can and should define their own womanhood. Because there are

one million different kinds of women, the third wave is big, and can get a little confusing and muddy, and maybe doesn't exist at all (history is a continuum, really, not a series of waves). Some of the new feminism—particularly the "I use my sexuality as a weapon!" crowd—can look a lot like the old sexism. But don't worry about it. Just follow your instincts and keep calling people on their shit.

POSTFEMINISM: SEXISM IS DEAD! LONG LIVE SEXISM!

Hhhhhhhhhhhhh. These dicks think that gender inequality is over and we should all have a party because *Sex and the City 2* was super empowering. Fuck these dicks. Or, rather, don't.

STOP VICTIM-BLAMING!

Repeat this one million times: When a person is raped, IT IS THE RAPIST'S FAULT.

STOP SLUT-SHAMING!

Women have the right to be sexual without guilt. Women can fuck as many people as they want. Women are not soiled or devalued by sexual activity or provocative clothing. Men, stop shaming women. Women, stop shaming yourselves. Honestly. This is just stupid.

GENDER IS A SOCIAL CONSTRUCT: WHAT *ARE* YOU!?

This is going to become mainstream thinking in the next few decades, so you might as well just get used to it. The idea is that gender roles are socially constructed—females do female things

because society tells them to, not because of the elusive "Cathy" gene (SHOE SHOPPING! ACK!). Also, a lot of people feel that they don't fit into the traditional binary concept of gender at all. (Important distinction: sex = biological/physical, gender = behavioral/societal.) Some people are biologically male but feel psychologically female. Some people feel like they're 75 percent male and 25 percent female, or 50 percent male and 50 percent female, or 150 percent dolphin, or whatever. Some people feel like they're none of the above. The bottom line is, other people's gender is 0 percent your business. People can identify however they like. Your male son can play with dolls. Your coworker can change her pronoun. Just calm down and be respectful and let people do their stuff.

WOMEN DO NOT EXIST FOR THE PURPOSES OF YOUR BONER

A lot of heterosexual men get very angry when women don't look the way they think women "should" look. But guess what? "Should" is not a thing. Women's bodies are none of your business. Women's body hair is none of your business. What women weigh is none of your business. What women wear is none of your business. Whether or not women want to fuck you is none of your business, unless they do want to fuck you, in which case you should go for it (high-five!).

MALE PRIVILEGE: IT IS REAL, AND IT IS TOTALLY BOGUS

Privilege is invisible. If you have no idea what male privilege is, there's a good chance you are currently benefiting from male privilege. That's how privilege works. Essentially, due to the social and political power structures that dominate the entire earth, shit is easier for men. Women make less money, exert less political influence, have their clitorises cut out (actually really truly—Google it), and are widely thought of as property and treated like poop. Privilege is real, and anyone who tells you otherwise is Ann Coulter.

A FINAL NOTE: YES, INDEED!

Unless you're a total asshat who thinks people are unequal, you are a feminist. YOU are a feminist. You ARE a feminist. YOU ARE A FEMINIST. Welcome aboard!

14. SOME FINANCIAL ADVICE COURTESY OF THE BIBLE

BY BETHANY JEAN CLEMENT AND CHRISTOPHER FRIZZELLE

Eschew Credit Cards

Y ou are young, you have no money, and you would like an electric guitar, a new iPhone, and a couch. But how will you afford these things? The credit card is among the greatest of college temptations. Beware the person with a clipboard in the quad, or the solicitations that come in the mail, because seeing one's name in raised plastic letters is one step toward hell.

Usury—defined by *Merriam-Webster's* as "the lending of money with an interest charge"—is a grave sin, listed in Ezekiel 22 alongside incest, murder, and beating up orphans.

It's a sin to borrow as well—"Leave off this usury," God warns the Jews in the book of Nehemiah, because debt corrupts—but more importantly, it's just a really stupid idea. You don't *have* any money, and borrowing money costs money, and borrowing money without any credit will cost you extra in interest, and the way it's rigged, you'll be paying off the interest on those credit cards forever and never actually be making a dent in what you owe—that's how the credit card companies make enough money to flood your mailbox with junk mail and fake credit cards and glossy brochures about far-off places you're never going to be able to afford once they swallow your life whole with ballooning credit card interest. If you already have a credit card, pay it on time and *always* pay more than the minimum. Whatever you do, don't take up day-trading while you have a credit card just because you see those commercials for day-trading on TV and think the stock market seems fun and easy and a great way to make enough money to pay off your credit cards. No! No stock market for you! Think of it this way: If you have 18 percent interest on a credit card, paying it off right away is like *making* 18 percent interest.

Plus, a paid-off credit card is great for your credit score, which means that later on in life, when you actually need credit, you'll get it with lower interest than you can get these days. It's what Jesus would do!

Get Thee Unto a Credit Union

Large banks suck. They don't care about you. This didn't used to be the case, but it became clear in 2008 that corporate banks didn't give a shit about inflicting ruinous financial bullshit on our country and, indeed, the world—first with the foreclosure crisis (they sold toxic investments as super-fucking-awesome investments and knew they were lying about it), and then with taxpayer-financed bailouts (which paid for taxpayer-financed super-fucking-awesome raises for all the guys at the top). If you're fully into screwing the lower 99 percent in favor of the top 1 percent of superrich assholes, by all means, join a big, douchey bank.

"The meek shall inherit the earth," the Bible says, but only if we fucking do something proactive. Get thee to a credit union, which are not-for-profit, member-owned co-ops that do not answer to Wall Street but to you. You will also receive better customer service and probably fewer charges for using your own goddamned money.

The Bible Further Suggests That You Get a Job

If you want to buy things, work. Remember Thessalonians: "If any would not work, neither should he eat." The wise college student takes this to heart by working in a place where he or she can eat for free. Waiting tables or otherwise working in a restaurant (see What No One Else Will Tell You About Working in Restaurants,

page 217) is the best way to make money and eat for free while doing so, but if you have no experience as a server, you may have to resort to lying (don't tell God!) or to pizza delivery or working in a movie theater. Working in a movie theater grants more social opportunities than pizza delivery, as well as plentiful popcorn. Communion with the world beyond the ivy-covered and/or graffiti-covered walls of your university is essential, because the pleasant dream of campus life will one day give way to the grinding tedium of your adult years. Get a taste of it now, and thou shalt appreciate thy time now more bountifully.

Jesus Christ on a Bicycle, Don't Buy a Car

And if you don't absolutely need the car you already have, sell it. Riding a bike is about $500 cheaper per month, and it makes your ass about 500 times hotter. Also, make your own coffee (see Make Your Own Coffee!, page 165). It's not that hard.

The Golden Rule and Beer

Follow the Golden Rule and you will be rewarded with so much GOLDEN BEER. The Golden Rule is, of course: Do unto others as you sure as hell wish they would do unto you. That means be nice and, if you're out on the town, tip well. Rewards await you—particularly if you revisit the same bar and let your high-tipping

self become known. However, the frugal college student knows to largely abstain from drinking in public houses, because the communion of the keg (or the similar sharing of other alcohol purchased from a store) is the way to satisfaction without the obliteration of the contents of one's wallet. For more on all of this, see What No One Else Will Tell You About Drinking, page 115.

15. HOW TO USE A COMPUTER

BY LINDY WEST

Things the Internet Is Good For (Now)

Masturbation, idle chatter with friends, jokes, laughs, chuckles, racism, dissemination of funny cat videos, the mocking of celebrities, gaining basic knowledge of almost any subject, passive-aggressive communication with one's mother, managing one's bank account, shopping, flirting, finding the closest Jamba Juice in one's zip code, etymology of words, spying on one's exes, spying on one's crushes, stealing massive amounts of media, murdering independent book and record stores, celebrity penis

research, 9/11 was an inside job, locating all the sex offenders within a five-block radius, looking up bus routes, looking up song lyrics, looking up driving directions, looking up what the sun is doing, locating humans with whom to have sex, checking one's flight status, figuring out the difference between houndstooth and windowpane check, collecting fake gold in a fake universe while dressed as a sexy elf, masturbation, masturbating one's genitals to completion, more masturbation, and masturbation.

Things the Internet Is Not Good For (Yet)

Genuine human connection, in-depth scholarly research, sustaining the human body with food and water, breaking up with a friend or lover, learning how to knit, feeling the life-giving warmth of the sun on one's skin, getting drunk, physical fitness, replacing electrolytes, tooth whitening, privacy, productivity, and not masturbating.

Trolls Be Trollin'

"BLUUUUUUHHHHHHHHHH! I'M AN INTERNET TROLL! FAT PEOPLE ARE THE FATTEST! GAY PEOPLE ARE GAY!!! GO BACK TO MEXICO, GAY PEOPLE!!! YOU'RE SO FAT THAT YOUR MOM'S SO FAT THAT SHE'S FAT! GUUUUURRRGGGG! I HIDE IN A BASEMENT AND HURT PEOPLE ON PURPOSE BECAUSE MY LIFE'S AMAZING!

SERIOUSLY, IT'S GOING EXACTLY AS PLANNED! BLACK PEOPLE SUCK! I HAVE AN INFECTIOUS SKIN DISEASE! I'M SO ALONE!!! GRAAAWWWW!!! FUCK JEWS!"

How to Twitter

Obviously you can do whatever you want with your Twitter, but really, stop writing about whatever mundane shit you're doing that day. Nobody cares. That's what Facebook is for. Nobody on Twitter cares that you had a cool time at Magic Mountain today. Nobody on Twitter needs to know that you bought a new shower curtain. Nobody on Twitter is like, "Holy shit! Jeff is eating *yogurt right now*!?!? RETWEETED." If you want to be the kind of Twitterer whom people on Twitter want to follow, CUT THAT SHIT OUT. No shower curtains, no roller coasters, no yogurt.

Twitter has three really useful uses: a tool for disseminating information from war-torn places where people are getting hit with sticks (e.g., "Ow! A policeman is hitting me with a stick!"), a way to alert people to interesting/funny/relevant content on the internet (e.g., "Peep this article, bro!"), and a global writer's room for hilarious people to hone their one-liner skills (e.g., "Chickens masturbate to cornography"). Everything else is boring and pointless.

How NOT to Facebook

No FarmVille, no Mafia Wars, no tagging people in unflattering photos, no frowny-face emoticons if someone dies (not that it should matter because NO DEATH ANNOUNCEMENTS ON FACEBOOK), no naked pictures, no deep emotions (awkward), no tagging a bunch of people in a picture of some fly Nikes, no making dinner plans (just use a PHONE).

Sexy, Sexy Pornos!!!

Look. Porn is great. Watch it or don't. But delete your browser history, okay? Please? Even if *you're* not embarrassed, the next person who uses that computer doesn't need the mental image of you fondling yourself to *Poontanglers 2: Last Tangle in Paris*. When it comes to porno, extremes are to be avoided. Nobody likes a militant anti-porn crazyperson, just like nobody likes a sweaty pornography addict. Just be normal. Use in moderation. Also avoid: kids, animals, dead bodies, nonconsenting adults.

SHOW ME YER BOOBZ

Some people really, really love the thrill of photographing their genitals and then transmitting said genitals electronically to the phones or e-mail accounts of potential or established sexual partners. Great. Fine. Go nuts. But seriously, NO FACE. Keep your face out of

it! No matter how much you think you can trust this person—clearly you trust them with your precious, precious gonads—remember that almost ALL relationships end. And when relationships end, things get sticky. And things could easily get extra sticky for you if your now-angry ex-beloved possesses a photo of you getting sticky all over your own face. KEEP THE FACE. OUT OF IT.

Also, dudes, pro tip: Establish whether or not a girl *wants* a picture of your penis *before* you send her a picture of your penis. Because maybe she does! But she probably doesn't. Really, she probably doesn't.

How to Un-Spam Thyself

Just never, ever enter passwords or personal information into any field on any website that you didn't seek out and go to on purpose. Nobody really has a free iPad for you. There is no Nigerian prince—Nigeria isn't even a monarchy. Your bank didn't send you an e-mail in broken English asking for your Social Security number because they "forgot it." Anything that looks like spam—even a little bit like spam—is spam. Delete, delete, delete.

How to Date People Inside Your Computer and Not Get Murdered

If you haven't noticed, we live in the future now. And in the future, online dating no longer carries that lonely-nerd-mom's-basement-wasteland

stigma that it used to have. It's normal now! Respectable! So date away! Meeting people online is just like meeting people in the real world, only without all the stuff that makes the real world real (you know, like trees and sunlight and vulnerability). Keep your profile short, light, and funny. Keep your pictures tame. Also: NO PHOTO OF YOU AND YOUR GUITAR. If you finally decide to take it to the next level, make sure to meet in a public place. (Pro tip: Right after you say, "Nice to meet you in person," say, "I'm so crazy-busy, I have to be somewhere in 45 minutes, I'm so sorry. How're you?" This establishes [1] that you have a life and [2] that you can leave in exactly 26 minutes if this person is zzzzzzzzzzzzzzz. If you end up liking them, you can say, "I'm just going to push this other thing back a half hour," and send a text to your houseplant about it. Do depart after that half hour. No big games, but this is a good time to leave them wanting more.) If someone seems like a murderer, politely decline a second date. Don't give out your Social Security number. And most importantly, NO UNSOLICITED PENIS PICTURES UNTIL DATE FIVE AT *LEAST*.

16. HOW TO WRITE GOOD

BY CHRISTOPHER FRIZZELLE

There is no secret to being a good writer. You have to read until your eyes bleed, write until your hands fall off, get new hands and eyeballs, and get back to it—you should be reading fiction, biographies, *The New Yorker*, the Sunday *New York Times*, *The Stranger*, poetry, essays, tell-alls, interviews, old stuff, new stuff, red stuff, blue stuff. Facebook and Twitter don't count—that's not writing, that's grunting. Read a few of the great comic campus novels—Kingsley Amis' *Lucky Jim*, Vladimir Nabokov's *Pnin*, Michael Chabon's *Wonder Boys*. The best books are funny: Feel free to put down any that aren't. Feel free to put down anything at any time. Life is 100 percent fatal, and you're not going to get to all the good stuff as it is.

Three Great Sentences and What Makes Them Great

A couple years ago, while visiting San Francisco, I saw something in a storefront window. It was a paragraph photocopied and enlarged into a huge poster, the letters fuzzy and weird. It was the first paragraph of F. Scott Fitzgerald's "The Crack-Up," an essay he wrote for *Esquire* 11 years after writing *The Great Gatsby* and four years before dying:

> Of course all life is a process of breaking down, but the blows that do the dramatic side of the work—the big sudden blows that come, or seem to come, from outside—the ones you remember and blame things on and, in moments of weakness, tell your friends about, don't show their effect all at once. There is another sort of blow that comes from within—that you don't feel until it's too late to do anything about it, until you realize with finality that in some regard you will never be as good a man again. The first sort of breakage seems to happen quick—the second kind happens almost without your knowing it but is realized suddenly indeed.

It's not every day you encounter a paragraph like this while you're walking down the street—who knows what it was doing there in that store window (San Francisco is magical). Fitzgerald's sentences are jolting, the way feeding a fork into an electric outlet is jolting,

and even though I'd read this paragraph in a book before, I stood there on the street jolting myself again and again, trying to figure out where the jolts come from. Later I wrote something on a blog about how "everything" you need to know about writing you can learn from that paragraph, which is kind of a stupid way to put it, although those sentences are packed with brilliance.

Should we do a close read?

"Of course all life is a process of breaking down" is great because the "Of course . . ." is so confidently conversational, hinting that what's coming is light and easy, or at least something we can all agree to, but then what comes is so morbid. You go into the sentence thinking you're going to get one thing, but right off you get something else, and it's startling. If a reader thinks they're going to get something in a sentence (or a character, or a plot) and then they do, they've been deposited into a cliché—which is not good writing. Good writing is: You think you're going to get one thing, but you don't.

The rhythm and the alliteration that come next ("but the blows," "do the dramatic") are good because they're subtle. They're there if you're listening, but they don't stand out. They don't put on tap shoes and go, "Hey everyone, check out how rhythmic and alliterative we're being!" They just sound nice. Likewise, several of the words echo ("blows" appears twice, "come" appears twice, "side" before "outside") without calling lots of attention to the echoing. The echoing just comes across as simplicity: Why reach for another word when what you mean is the word you just used?

And—to keep going—making the words echo echoes the prevailing point about getting older, because the idea of an echo contains the idea of lapsed time. (A word appears early [in life/in the sentence] and then it appears again later [in life/in the sentence].)

Another thing to marvel at (drool over) in that first sentence: the economy of "the ones you remember." Makes you think of all the blows you've forgotten, without mentioning them. "And, in moments of weakness, tell your friends about" is an unexpected, funny, and concise critique of his friends, evoking a loneliness that would be maudlin to spell out. And "don't show their effect all at once" is the sentence's payoff, the final whiplash, which leaves so much unsaid, raises more questions, and draws you further in. Those seven words—"don't show their effect all at once"—give off a funny feeling every time you read them, a funny feeling in the chest, like you're being lifted up by them. You get this same feeling at the end of a lot of great first sentences. (Check out the first sentence of Joan Didion's essay "Insider Baseball" sometime.)

After all the subtle showing off of that first sentence, we get a very regular second sentence, not a complicated one or an alliterative one or one where the grammar echoes the meaning or whatever—it's just strong and blunt. Fitzgerald's saying: I realize that first sentence was super rich, have a glass of water now. It comes as a relief, and yet it's very much in the mood of the first sentence, so there's no interruption.

Then there's the third sentence with that insane em dash. As you know if you read Fitzgerald, he believed you can never be

too rich or have too many em dashes. Notice how the em dash in the third sentence doesn't function like em dashes usually do—at least it doesn't function like the em dashes in the first and second sentences do. "The first sort of breakage seems to happen quick—the second kind happens almost without your knowing it but is realized suddenly indeed." On any planet, that em dash should be a semicolon. Or it should be a period. But those would slow you down, whereas that em dash is like a people mover at the airport: It slides you forward without you doing anything. It speeds you up, sending you right into the next thought, almost too quickly, against your will, as if you're trapped in the forward-moving-ness of, well, you know, life, and getting older, and the process of breaking down, in spite of your every wish.

What Not to Do

DON'T USE CLICHÉS

Clichés are useless, and they're everywhere. Since everyone knows them already, there's no point in writing them down. If you want to make the point that "you never know what it's like to walk in someone else's shoes," you have more thinking to do, because SHUT UP. It's a cliché. It's hokey. It's boring. The secret to good writing is that it's interesting, and used-up, dried-out, shopworn thoughts and phrases are not interesting.

DON'T WASTE TIME

The other thing about clichés is they waste time, and good writing doesn't waste time. Describing the sky as "blue" is wasting time; describing someone as "quiet as a mouse" is three words longer than necessary; don't write "as a rule of thumb" when you just mean "as a rule"; and never, ever write "for all intents and purposes." You don't want any words in your writing that don't need to be there; they're just junking up the place. Likewise, don't use a long word when a short word will do. Long words are florid and showy and annoying. In that Fitzgerald paragraph quoted earlier, he uses "blows" instead of "calamities" or "letdowns" or "afflictions," and then repeats "blows" instead of reaching for a synonym, and the paragraph is so much better—sharper, more memorable—because of it.

DON'T OVERWRITE

Don't use "utilize," just use "use." Only douchebags and blowhards use "utilize." As mentioned above, finding a synonym for the word you just used doesn't make the next sentence better; it makes the next sentence overwritten. Don't write "murmured" or "exclaimed" or "rejoined" when "said" works; come to think of it, always use "said," no matter what. Anything other than "said" is desperate, thesaurus-y. I didn't "pen" this chapter that you're reading right now, I "wrote" it.

DON'T USE FIRST PERSON UNLESS YOU HAVE TO

Speaking of being annoying, don't write "I" into sentences you don't need to be in. "I think that movie is terrible" is not as good a sentence as "That movie is terrible"—the meaning's the same, it's clear an opinion is being given, but one's got filler and the other doesn't. Plus, "I think that movie is terrible" has a whiff of self-importance to it, as if we are supposed to know/care who this "I" is. (The people who write "I" a lot are the kind of people who always want to tell you about their dreams.) Finding ways to avoid self-importance is a useful challenge for a writer: You couldn't get more self-important than that weepy paragraph by Fitzgerald about falling apart, and yet it doesn't stink with self-importance because it doesn't have the word "I" in it. Go ahead and use "I" if it makes a sentence funnier or if there's just no way to write the sentence without the "I" because, say, you fell down a flight of stairs. You can't really improve on the sentence "Then I fell down a flight of stairs."

How to Write a College Paper

Because so many people have potatoes where their brains should be—no matter how many times they hear something or see something, they don't get it, they have nothing to say, they have no questions, hhhhhhhhhhh—because of these people, the college paper was invented. It's to separate the potatoes-for-brains from people with the capacity to absorb information, apply it to other

things they know about, and express a response. That's all you're doing with a college paper. You're saying, *I learned a thing, and here's what's interesting about it.*

You do this with sentences and paragraphs. If you have a question/prompt, give a confident answer (in the first paragraph) and support your point with examples/evidence (each one getting its own paragraph—what the example is and how it supports what you're saying). Then, at the end, restate your point and why it's interesting. And you're done. If you don't have a question to answer—if you're in a literature class and you're just supposed to respond critically to a text—well, that's a fun one. That just means: *Show off how you think.* Go crazy. Come up with a specific question and then take a look at how the text answers it, and show your work, once again with each example getting its own paragraph.

Reread your writing—preferably after letting it sit overnight or at least for an hour or two. Ways to make it better will be obvious.

Don't bore your teacher. Imagine how many boring papers that poor person has to read.

How to Write a Cover Letter

You're overthinking this. You just write it like a normal person. Keep it short. Shorter. No clichés, no wasting time, no overwriting. Try not to be funny—*trying* to be funny is the worst in a cover letter. Keep it just: Here's who you are, here's why you're writing. Then reread it. Did you reread it? It's full of typos. REREAD IT!

The Stranger received a cover letter by e-mail from someone who wanted to write a sports column. The subject line: "The Starnger Needs a sport's Writer." That person is not going to get a response. Likewise, cool it on the superlatives about how thrilled you are at the possibility of maybe getting an interview, because you're just going to sound like a freak. You'll end up like the poor woman who once sent a cover letter we've been reading aloud in the office ever since—a letter we framed and hung on a wall.

It begins, "Your newspaper is brilliant, professional, progressive, enlightening, edgy, and so bitingly human that I could swear it bleeds." Aw, that's nice—she reads the paper and she likes it. Good to know. "All in all it offers the well blended and well aged voice that a modern audience craves. It is a staple in my Seattle apartment and I have been known to send sections of it back East to friends and devotees with great frequency." Okay, so she reads it a lot, and likes it a lot. "*The Stranger* has seamlessly tapped into the pulse of Seattle and has thus developed Seattle's fingerprints and nuances." Like, a lot a lot. "It is everything an alternative city newspaper should be." Uh huh. "That is why I am at the cusp of my excitement to be your intern."

Those quotes are just from the first paragraph.

There are five paragraphs.

She goes on to state that working at a college publication "allowed me to fertilize the skill set necessary to create fluidity when pinned to the wall, poise when encountering formidable challenge, and consistency when working amongst chaos." She adds, "My work

ethic and devotion to professional development are irremovable aspects of my personality." A few sentences later, she writes, "If these notations speak to anything I would hope they speak to the severity of my desire."

Then, later: "In addition to my vivacity, dedication, and competence, my personal symphony of written voice and exhaustless creativity should be highlighted. I offer them to you because I envision our relationship as being extremely mutually rewarding. I would be honored to invest in your riveting and entertaining journal. Please contact me at your earliest convenience . . . "

No one ever did. Sometimes we wonder whatever happened to her, although we don't wonder very much.

How to Write Poetry

Do you know who Emily Dickinson was? Do it like that.

17. WHAT NO ONE ELSE WILL TELL YOU ABOUT HEARTBREAK AND DEATH

BY BETHANY JEAN CLEMENT AND CHRISTOPHER FRIZZELLE

I t is inevitable: Someone is going to break your heart, and someone you love is going to die (followed, inevitably, by another person, then another, etc.—hopefully not in close succession). It's not going to be pretty, but you will get through it.

How to Get Over a Broken Heart

There's baby-games sad-because-it's-over, then there's the real deal: Heart. Break. True heartbreak is unmistakable, because it hurts so much. It hurts like being sick—it hurts like you're going to die. Nothing means anything, nothing is worth anything, because they don't love you. If you're not the stoic type, you have to carry Kleenex around because you never know when you're going to start crying. If you're the stoic type, the tears you don't cry hurt just as much as the ones you do.

But there is something—one thing—that will help. That thing is time. You'll feel better with time. You don't believe it right now. You think you'll never get over this; you think you'll never feel better; you are in the depths of despair, and you will dwell forever there. Not so, friend. Time heals all wounds, even the broken heart.

How much time? Some people maintain that for every year you were together, you must suffer through one month of heartbreak. But even if you were together for only six months, you've still got some hurt before you start feeling better. If you were only together for a couple months, you may feel heartbroken, but you'll probably realize later you really didn't even know the person, and, conversely, they really didn't know you. Which is somewhat comforting.

Even if you were together for months and months, you might still find out later you had no idea what was going on. Say, for instance, your first love, clearly the love of your life—the person who loves old movies like you do, and is so funny, and who writes

you love letters that you read over and over, and whose beautiful eyes you would live inside if such a thing were possible—breaks up with you, and you carry Kleenex everywhere, and you feel like you want to die. You call your mom—that's how messed-up you feel—and your mom says, "Oh, honey. I'm so, so sorry. But you'll feel better with time." You cry some more, because you know in your extremely broken heart that she's wrong, that a human being cannot recover from pain like this. But she's right, and after you spend every hour of every day questioning what's wrong with you and how can you be so unlovable and what did you do wrong and missing missing missing crying crying crying—eventually, slowly, you feel better. You're shocked, but you really do. Fast-forward 10 years. You live in a different city. You have a pretty neat job. You've loved again! It's like a miracle when it happens. And now you are or you aren't seeing someone or in love or what have you. You hear from your heartbreaker—the first one, the one with the eyes—that they're going to be in town and that your old mutual friend Philip is having a party and it's an hour or so outside of town and do you want to drive there together? Sure you do. A part of you wonders, with a very real thrill, what might be rekindled; you remember the love you had for this person with a vividness that seems somewhat impossible, after all this time. The first time you met, and how they looked in the half light of the night outside the party, how crazily happy you were every time you saw them, the time you rolled around together in the still-warm sand. But when you get together now, riding in the car, just the two of you, your heartbreaker has lost

their spark completely. Your heartbreaker starts talking about back then, and how much they drank, and how serious that was. "What?" you say. "Do you mean like you drank secretly?" you ask. Yes, that is what your heartbreaker means. You can't quite believe this. Your heartbreaker goes on and on about themselves back then—and themselves now, and themselves in between—with you thinking all the while about how preposterous it sounds. How could you not have known this person you used to love had a secret drinking problem? And: If only you'd known! This is total vindication! It really wasn't your fault! You wish so, so much that yourself back then—the self you also remember entirely vividly, carrying Kleenex around and wanting to die, your poor, sweet, younger self—could have known this. At the same time, you're having another realization: You never really knew this other person at all. The mind reels. Can you ever truly know what's in another person's heart? This is crazy. Your heartbreaker is still talking and now is saying that as part of their 12-step program, they're making amends to those they hurt, way back a decade ago, and they want to make amends to you. "That was a long time ago," you say. "You don't have to do that," you say. "It doesn't matter anymore," you say—and with a pleasant shock, you realize that you absolutely mean it. But yes, your heartbreaker says, they *do* have to do this, it's important, and on and on and on. You repeat yourself: long time ago, not important, water under the proverbial bridge. Your heartbreaker clearly wants some very specific verbiage from you about accepting the amends-making, but the whole thing seems more about your heartbreaker than anyone

or anything else. You're on the side of your past self—the poor, sweet, heartbroken thing. So you never actually say you accept the amends. And it isn't until more years go by that you do—you accept, and you say it out loud, to an empty room.

But let's back up: Your heart is broken. Only time will really help, but friends help a little. You might only be able to see them hazily through your pain, but spend time with them. They might bring you ice cream. (Note that when a friend of yours is heartbroken, you should be so, so nice to them, and also bring them ice cream. And refrain from too much I-told-you-so if you never liked the person they were with in the first place.) Meanwhile, it's okay to dwell in bed for limited periods of time, but go outside. Take walks. Stay busy. Do something nice for someone else.

If you really can't get out of bed—can't go to class or work or function at all normally—call a friend or your mom or a mental health help line and get some help. Likewise, if you fall into self-destructive behavior—too many drugs, or unprotected sex, or anything like that—get some help.

As a wise man once said, it gets better. The first time your heart is broken, it seems unfixable. The good news is, you're stronger than you think. And chances are, that person was kind of a shitheel in ways you don't even know, and not right for you at all. Just hold on. You'll see.

When Someone You Love Dies

If you think a regular old broken heart is painful, try this one on for size. You will never see this person again—the finality is unbelievable, in the sense that it cannot be believed. The devastation seems complete. Many great minds have tried to address this pain, but there is not much to say. Only time will help. Some say that it takes a year to begin to feel normal again after losing someone very close to you.

But meanwhile, know that every single thing you loved about this person still lives on within you.

On Suicide

Please do not do that. If you're thinking about suicide, you need to know that you will feel better. It doesn't seem like it—it seems impossible—but you will feel better. Problems that seem insurmountable have solutions. Reach out to someone right away; call a friend or a suicide hotline (1-800-273-8255). You WILL get through this; you WILL feel better. Life is worth living. Hold on, and get some help.

APPENDIX A. WHAT NO ONE ELSE WILL TELL YOU ABOUT WORKING IN RESTAURANTS

At some point or another, if you have hands and eyeballs and a cell phone bill, you'll probably work in a restaurant. If you're lucky and you're good at it, you might end up waiting tables in a fine-dining establishment, like Dan Savage did. If you're good at faking it, you'll end up waiting tables for a giant chain, like Christopher Frizzelle did. If you vaguely know your way around a stove, you might end up working in the kitchen, like Bethany Jean Clement did. And if you're not cut out for waiting tables or cooking,

you might end up squeezing orange juice or doing janitorial duty, like Lindy West and Brendan Kiley did—although neither did either for long.

In a certain sense, all restaurant jobs are the same: Your boss sucks, your customers are entitled jerks, and your coworkers are the best. Your coworkers are the reason that restaurant jobs can be so fun—it's like you're all putting on a show together. And then after work, everyone gets drunk together and talks shit about the owner, the dishwashers, the clientele. Oh, the shit that is talked! Whether you work in a restaurant for a few months or the rest of your life, you will be retelling your restaurant stories for the rest of time. And you will learn things you won't learn any other way.

What It's Like Working for a Mom-and-Pop Bakery

. . . .

BY LINDY WEST

After college, I lived in a sagging, blue, house-shaped pile of mice in Los Angeles. The house was on Silver Lake Boulevard (on the shitty side of Sunset), and I lived there with three friends, a basenji with bowel-control problems, one million black widow spiders, an eternally wasted landlord with "power-mad dreams" (his words) living in the basement, and a trio of fashion designers upstairs who would frequently wake us at 3 a.m. by roller-skating in circles around what I can only assume was a Matterhorn of cocaine. It was the funnest place I have ever lived.

I needed to find a job if I was going to stay in LA. Just a few blocks down Silver Lake Boulevard (nice side of Sunset) was a bakery. They had great fried-egg sandwiches! And they were hiring! I worked there for exactly six hours.

Instead of a traditional job interview, the owners told me, they liked to have potential employees work a "trial day" in the bakery. This is the kind of scam that a family-run place can get away with. For my time and trouble, I would receive zero dollars, one fried-egg sandwich, and—potentially—a job. I said sure. I arrived. They put me to work in a back room preparing their very popular fresh-squeezed orange juice. The Backdoor Bakery went through many, many gallons of fresh-squeezed orange juice every day. Math fact: The number of oranges required to make one gallon of fresh-squeezed orange juice is eleventy grillion. Backdoor Bakery fact: All of those oranges were juiced BY HAND. SPECIFICALLY, MY FUCKING HAND. There was an "electric" juicer, but it only "worked" if you leaned into it mightily at an arm-torquing angle. I juiced and juiced and juiced for hours. I sweated, I groaned, my limbs cramped. Then, suddenly, I found myself momentarily alone in the room with the employee who had trained me on the juicer. She approached me quickly and quietly. "Get out," she whispered. "Run. Don't work here. Run. Get OUT."

In the end, it didn't matter, because the Backdoor Bakery never called me back. Apparently my free labor wasn't up to snuff. I moved back to Seattle a couple months later. I really miss those fried-egg sandwiches.

What It's Like Working for a Chain Restaurant

BY CHRISTOPHER FRIZZELLE

At a desperate point in my life, I answered a cattle call for open positions at a soon-to-open chain restaurant out in the suburbs. Since I didn't own a car, I had to bus it. The interview process involved a written multiple-choice personality test like nothing I'd ever seen before—pages of probing hypothetical questions meant to gauge how out-of-your-mind thrilled you were to put on your pants every morning. Questions like "Do you ever have plans to go on a romantic date but then cancel because you're doubting yourself?" All my answers said: *Absolutely not! Never! Feelings are for losers!*

I got the job.

They may call it a "personality test," but it's more like they're testing for an absence of personality, which makes sense considering how programmed every second of the chain-restaurant experience is. Your uniform will vary, but at this particular restaurant I had to wear a bright white shirt, a bright white apron, bright white pants, and bright white shoes—since I'm six foot five, I looked like the Stay Puft Marshmallow Man—and say the things they trained you to say in the order they trained you to say them. Since I'd never actually been a server, this was helpful. (It's well-known in the restaurant world that most servers lied to get their first server job; I had a friend who worked at another restaurant give me a

reference.) I had to learn the exact titles of all the items on the billion-page menu, and identify dishes based on slides, and be able to tell customers which ones had cilantro in them, and recite which beers were on tap and what the well vodka and whiskey were, all of which was a pain, yes, but once you had it down, you were set.

The stressful part was the computer watching everything constantly. You had to say a certain thing to a new table within 30 seconds of them sitting down and something else within two minutes. If a table didn't get their food within another certain number of minutes, the computer alerted a manager, who then became involved. Stressful as it was for the server, the upside was a very focused level of service—a level of service customers don't always get at "fancy" restaurants. The downside was that not every customer wants a focused level of service. Sometimes customers want to plant a flag, start a colony, and live at their table forever.

And, of course, the customer pretty much gets to do whatever they want. One time, late in the evening, a couple said something like "We've planted a flag, we're starting a colony, we're going to live here forever—you don't have to keep checking in on us." Since they wanted me to stop hovering and since I still had a chance of catching the earlier bus, I started in on my side work, which that evening involved walking into a refrigerator the size of my apartment and pouring ranch dressing from a giant square vat into a tiny round hole. The square vat and the round hole at the top of the dressing pourer were clearly not made by the same person, so it took some doing, and by the time I reemerged from the walk-in freezer, the

manager looked at me like I'd killed and eaten his children. Turns out, that one last table had changed their mind while I was in the freezer and decided they wanted to leave, and they had to flag down a manager to ring up their bill. The manager had droopy eyes and the humorlessness of a career chain-restaurant night manager, and he had very detailed rhetoric about what I'd done wrong. He got out some paperwork and wrote me up, and had me read what he'd written and then sign it, because big chain restaurants are not about human interactions—they're about rules and timers and paperwork. But when you need a job, you need a job, and you swallow your pride and give in. I signed his stupid piece of paper and then walked to a bus station, dressed head to toe in white, to wait for the late bus home.

What It's Like Working for a High-End Restaurant in London

BY DAN SAVAGE

I owe Jonathan Waxman an apology.

No, wait: I owe the people who bought Jams of London from Jonathan Waxman an apology. Or I owe them two or three thousand dollars—and, hey, does anyone know what the statute of limitations is for grand theft? In the UK?

Jonathan Waxman "is an American chef who was one of the pioneers of California cuisine," says Wikipedia. He opened a restaurant in New York City called Jams in the early 1980s. It was

his second restaurant, and it was a huge success—Jams got name-checked in the 1987 Diane Keaton yuppie/ovary anxiety flick *Baby Boom*—and a couple years later Waxman opened Jams of London. I moved to London in 1988 and, through a friend of a friend of a friend, got a job waiting tables there.

Jams of London was an American-owned, American-style restaurant, but a pricey one, and it featured "American-style service." It was a style of service—four-star but with an air of casual informality—that Brits just couldn't do. Local waiters had two gears: lickspittle servility or barely concealed hostility. Consequently, the waiting jobs at Jams mostly went to American expats.

The clientele was moneyed—film and television stars, business execs, the odd (sometimes very odd) lord or lady—and the money was outstanding: A 15 percent gratuity was added to every check (American food, American service, American tips), and the waiters split the take at the end of the night. Jams of London was a great gig, and everyone who worked there realized how lucky they were and busted their asses for Jams, for Jonathan, for each other.

But like all really good restaurant gigs . . . it couldn't last. Waxman sold Jams of London to a bounder who owned a rib joint off Trafalgar Square, and the new owner immediately revised the tipping policy: A 15 percent gratuity was still added to every check, but the money was no longer distributed to the waiters. All tips went straight into the pocket of the new owner, a man who had a large estate in the country to look after.

The new owner should've fired the entire staff and started over, but the place would've collapsed. So we were all kept on. Only now, instead of a group of highly motivated American expats who were grateful to the owners and wanted Jams to succeed, Jams of London was staffed by a group of seething, unmotivated angerbombs who hated the new owner and couldn't wait for Jams to fail.

Here's the thing about screwing over your employees: They find ways to screw you right back.

Which brings me to the flatware at Jams of London. The place had amazing silver—Christofle? Have you heard of it?—and before every shift, we waiters would sit and polish each spoon, soup spoon, fork, salad fork, knife, and bread knife. One day, while I sat with another waiter in the dining room before the dinner shift, I polished one fork for Jams, one for myself, one knife for Jams, one for myself, dropping each piece of silverware I polished for myself into a backpack at my feet. I left Jams that day with 12 settings—72 pieces of silver—which I still have and haul out (and polish!) at Thanksgiving and Christmas.

Just the spoons—in the pattern Jams had and I have—cost $118 apiece. I discovered that a few years ago when I decided to replace one of the spoons, which I'd lost in a move, and Googled "Christofle."

$118. For a spoon.

Jams wasn't long for London, and neither was I. Three months after making off with thousands of dollars' worth of silverware, I was back in the United States, and on to my next restaurant gig: making milk shakes for sorority girls in Illinois.

What It's Like Working as a Restaurant Janitor

. . . .

BY BRENDAN KILEY

One summer, I worked as a night janitor at a bakery. Everybody wound up regretting it. I regretted having to go to work at 8 p.m., as my friends were all just going out for the night, and I regretted spending the next several hours mopping and shoving disgusting rubber floor mats into industrial dishwashers. My employers regretted that they didn't put their cache of nitrous oxide under lock and key.

If you are the kind of person who's easily bored, I don't recommend janitorial work. I tried to relieve the boredom of the job each night by putting on music and taking occasional hits of nitrous—we called it "hippie crack" back then. One night, while suffering a strong attack of youthful ennui (and its attendant selfishness), I went on a full-blown nitrous bender. I sat cross-legged on the floor, behind the counter so nobody could see me through the windows, with boxes of nitrous canisters and the bakery's whipped-cream dispenser. I commenced to huffing in as much nitrous oxide as my poor body and brain could manage. I had put on some music (can't remember what, but it could've been Dinosaur Jr., Sonic Youth, or maybe even some of the Grateful Dead's folky/country stuff—those bands were in heavy rotation that summer) and eventually woke up to the sound of music while I stared at the ceiling.

I figured they were going to fire me. They did. Huffing nitrous

at your restaurant job isn't a good idea if you want to keep your restaurant job.

I didn't really care, and soon afterward got my first newspaper job, at the local community paper, covering school boards and city council and land use and other boring stuff. But it wasn't nearly as boring as mopping that goddamned bakery floor.

What It's Like Working as a Barista, an Incompetent Waitress, a Barely Competent Cook, and at a Shady Café

BY BETHANY JEAN CLEMENT

My first job ever was at a French bakery called La Boulangerie. It was owned by a diminutive but elegant European couple; he played the bassoon, professionally somehow, even though Americans barely knew what the bassoon was. I worked all day Saturdays behind the counter, all through senior year of high school. Work started at the ungodly hour of 7 a.m., and when I first started, I didn't like coffee.

Within a few weeks, my coworker and I were having espresso-shot-drinking contests. By the time we closed up at the end of the day, we were pretty much mopping the ceiling to the *Benny Hill* theme song. The coffee also helped if I was hungover from a keg party, as did a little lie-down in the back on the cool tile floor. I loved making coffee drinks—the buzz of the machine, the hiss of

the steam—and did it exactingly: Don't run the shots too long, don't scald the milk. At the beginning, I'd surreptitiously dip my finger in to make sure the milk was hot enough; later, I realized you could just feel the side of the little stainless steel pitcher.

The true greatness of the Boulangerie was the paradise of pastry. I was always so hungry—so, so hungry. An abiding hunger lived inside me. It was smash-downable with a dose of food, but then it would come roaring back just a few hours later: HONNN-GRY! FOOOOOOOOD! I was two-dimensionally thin, to the extent that my parents worried I was anorexic, and I could eat and eat and barely make a dent in the Boulangerie's trays full of golden croissants, the pillows of brioche, the sugar-crisped palmiers, and the little shell-shaped madeleines.

The taste of all the burnished baked goods is like a muscle memory, I can run my mind over them and compare every baked good ever to their perfection. A proper ham and cheese croissant, made with Gruyère, heated up (convection or regular oven, NEVER microwave) remains my primary love, still. Occasionally, someone would special-order a Brie en brioche or a honey-almond tart, then (unthinkably) never show up to retrieve it: heaven. At the end of the day, anything left over was ours—bagsful of baguette and raisin-studded escargot and pithivier.

Sometimes, people would call and say they'd found a rubber band in their croissant or—one time, truly—a Band-Aid in their baguette. "That is *terrible*," we would say mournfully. "But you must mean La Petite Boulangerie. They're a Pepsi-Cola chain. This is La

Boulangerie—we are a family-owned, authentic French bakery."
Your spine straightened reflexively as you said this, and you gazed
nobly into the middle distance. This was the feeling of justified pride.

In college, I went to see about a job at the Ingleneuk Tea House.
It was a stodgy restaurant in a Victorian house; its claim to fame
was that James Michener had worked there when he was a student,
which seemed like a poor one. They took me on as a waitress,
despite the fact that I had a terrible memory and couldn't carry
things. I worked for one shift, during most of which I hid from my
trainer, folding and refolding white cloth napkins, terrified to go out
on the floor. The shift meal was substandard turkey and mashed
potatoes and gravy, with canned cranberry sauce. I hope I called to
say I wasn't coming back; I don't remember at all. The Ingleneuk
later burned down.

After graduation, I was back in Seattle with the world's most
expensive bachelor's degree in English literature, unemployed. I
happened to go to a bar called the Roanoke one afternoon for a
beer, and I got to talking to a friend of a friend, who turned out to
be one of the owners, and by the time I left I had a job as a cook in
the Roanoke's tiny kitchen. I had no experience. This is the kind of
thing that happens at the Roanoke.

It was just simple stuff: sandwiches, nachos. I'm sure the nice
owner-man thought: Any fool can do this job. I did eventually attain
competence, if that may be measured by people no longer sending
their food back because the cheese wasn't melted. But I never quite
got the extremely basic triangulation of making each and every

thing as delicious as possible for other people just as you would for yourself at home. Also, if I got more than one order, I felt like I was falling behind, all alone, doomed; I just didn't have anywhere near the nerve for working in a kitchen.

I did learn the best way to cut an avocado, and how to pull a tap beer with a snap, and to never, ever take a drink from a man before it was completely, incontrovertibly empty—I almost lost a hand a couple times that way at the Roanoke. The jolly bartender Tom would go out back to "play ping-pong," leaving me behind the bar, and the guys who drank there in the afternoons teased me, and I was shy, which made it even better sport. Once when I was back in the kitchen five minutes before the end of my shift, the phone rang—an order for 20 hot sandwiches, to go. "*Tommmmmmm!*" I wailed, sticking my head out. All the guys all along the bar laughed uproariously, especially the one still on the other end of the line.

My last food job was in San Francisco. It was at a café that paid under the table; I lived in a room that was meant to be a closet, so I'd be able to get by. The café is gone, and for the life of me, I can't remember the name. I worked with the immigrant brother of the immigrant owner, who treated his brother more like a dog. But the owner wasn't around much, and the brother and I got along. He was taking ESL classes, and when we weren't busy, I helped him with his reading.

But there was the matter of the ravioli. I didn't even know we served ravioli until someone ordered it. I asked the brother about the ravioli. "Ah!" he said, and started burrowing in the

glass-doored refrigerator. He went so far back that he all but disappeared. Eventually he emerged with a metal hotel pan with dripping, opaque plastic wrap over it. He unwrapped it to reveal a school of gray ravioli suspended in fetid water. "We can't serve that!" I whispered. "Oh, no, no, no, it's okay," he said, and fetched a colander and dumped the ravioli into it in the sink. He started running cold water over the ravioli, rinsing away the visible gray skin on each one. "NO!" I said, louder. "It's okay! It's okay!" he said. "NO IT IS NOT OKAY! WE CAN'T SERVE THAT!" I said, loud enough for customers out at the tables to hear. We went back and forth for a bit, but I put my foot down, and I made him throw it away in front of me.

A little while after that, a regular at the café was talking about his new internet company, and it turned out there was a great job for an English literature major there. I called the owner to tell him I had to quit, that I was getting my shifts covered—he interrupted me with a stream of invective I've not heard the likes of before or since. "I GIVE YOU THIS FUCKING JOB AND THIS IS WHAT YOU DO TO ME!" He went on and on, cursing fabulously and liberally. It was insane, but he was a grown-up, and I was shaking with an animal fear. Finally, he paused in his rage, and suddenly I knew what to do. "NO, FUCK YOU!" I said, and hung up the phone.

APPENDIX B.
THE DIFFERENT KINDS OF
PEOPLE THAT THERE ARE

BY LINDY WEST

PEOPLE WHO CHOOSE TO CORRECT YOU ABOUT THE DEFINITION OF "HOBO"

Am I making this up? I feel like every time someone uses the word "hobo" to mean "homeless person," somebody else has to climb waaay up on their high horse and don their semantics cap and start getting highfalutin all over town about how "a hobo is someone who rides the rails in the Great Depression, and is it 1934 right now? I don't think so! And I can't believe you don't even know what words mean. How embarrassing. Have you heard of

Wikipedia? Hhhhhhhhhhhhh." Maybe I'm making all of this up, but if I'm not, I'd just like to say that I'm aware of what year it is, and I am going to continue using the word "hobo" however I please (within reasonable homeless-related limits, of course), thank you very much, and the way in which I please to use it is, "No thank you, hobo, I do not wish to go on a date with you." Also I will accept "transient."

PEOPLE WHO ARE MEAN TO HOBOES

Lay off, man. Being homeless is the worst thing. Give the dude a dollar. (I'm still not going on a date with you, hobo.)

PEOPLE WHO STILL HAVE JOBS

As bad as things are, this is still most people. People with jobs are great, except for the few who talk shit to people without jobs (things like "Hey, get a job!" or "Where's your job?"). In such instances, these people need to be reminded that they, too, possess jobs vulnerable to layoffs and should probably shut the fuck up.

PEOPLE WHO ARE QUIETLY LESS THAN $100 AWAY FROM COMPLETE DESTITUTION

You have to hope it's going to be okay. This can't go on forever.

PEOPLE WHO SECRETLY HAVE VAST FAMILY FORTUNES/TRUST FUNDS TO KEEP THEM FROM EVER KNOWING COMPLETE DESTITUTION, OR EVEN MILD HARDSHIP

Just do something interesting with it. You already won. Be grateful. Don't be a douche.

PEOPLE WHO CLAIM TO BE AFRAID OF CLOWNS

These people (and they are numerous) are attempting to cultivate a cute quirk, but they are really just aping a cute quirk cultivated by thousands of cute-quirk-cultivators before them in a giant, gross, boring feedback loop. Yes, clowns can be mildly creepy. But come *on*. Among the many things that are scarier than clowns: fire, earthquakes, a guy with a knife, riding the bus, colon cancer, falling down the stairs (it could happen at any time!), rapists, people who just kind of look a little rapey and are standing too close to you in line at 7-Eleven, Marlo from *The Wire*, influenza, and scissors.

PEOPLE WHO DON'T WATCH TV

Symbolically not doing something for the sake of not doing it is almost never evidence of sophistication. It is evidence of not knowing what you're fucking talking about. Are we really still having this conversation? Television is a part of the cultural landscape at this point—a lot of it is good. A lot of it is bad, some of which is also good. You know, LIKE ALL THINGS MADE BY HUMANS? Obviously it is also a good idea to go outside once in a while. But the presence

of a television in your home does not make that decision for you. You make it. Feel free to still go outside at any time.

PEOPLE WHO WILL JUST HAVE A BITE OF WHATEVER YOU'RE HAVING

Please, please, please just order your own lasagna.

PEOPLE WHO STUDIED ABROAD IN A THIRD-WORLD COUNTRY

Congratulations.

PEOPLE WHO ARE INTO WHIMSY

You can't really be mad at people who send away for porcelain figurines of poodles wearing poodle skirts that they saw in the back of *PARADE*, or who enjoy movies in which impish children attempt to call grandma in heaven on the CB radio. That'd be like punching Helen Keller in the face. These people just want to be left alone with their extremely lifelike baby replicas—small false humans filled with pretend love that can be asphyxiated with attention and never poop, cry, or grow up to make fun of anyone's stretch pants and doily collection. Forever-babies. (Note: Sometimes people who are into whimsy are *not* into things like gay marriage. In which case, fuck 'em.)

PEOPLE WHO ARE WHITE WHO CALL BLACK PEOPLE "BROTHAS" WHEN TALKING TO OTHER WHITE PEOPLE, AS IN, "A LOT OF MY FRIENDS ARE BROTHAS"

These embarrassing people have lots of black friends and are very comfortable around black people. They also aren't weirded out about being at the gay bar because their ex-girlfriend was bisexual.

PEOPLE WHO ARE OLD

Notable old people include: Methuselah, George Burns, Andy Rooney, an elephant, Dick Van Dyke, Slade Gorton the senator, Father Time, Slade Gorton the Gorton's fisherman, John McCain's mom, the old lady who dropped it into the ocean at the end, Harrison Ford.

OLD PEOPLE WHO THINK PIGEONS ARE THEIR BEST FRIENDS

Listen, old people. Pigeons do not love you. Much like robots and the British, pigeons do not have the capacity to feel love. They only have the capacity to desire croutons. And when you spread infinity croutons across the grass outside MY house, for the purpose of making pigeons love you (WHICH WILL NEVER HAPPEN), the only result is infinite feces. I now have to walk upon feces-encrusted streets through a feces-encrusted world. Because of you and your delusions of pigeon love. Stop it.

BABIES

The opposite of old people. They are like you and me, except smaller, more illiterate, and with less money.

PEOPLE WHO ARE SECRET HOOKERS

They're your friends, but they're *hookers*! Ssssh!

RECESSION HOOKERS

No judging. Sometimes these things happen. There but for the grace of writing a bunch of bullshit go I.

PEOPLE WHO ARE PRETTY *AND* SMART *AND* FUNNY *AND* NICE

You probably want to hate these people, but why bother? They are absolutely wonderful, and all we can do is deal with it and hope to be charming enough that they will someday mate with us so that our children can absorb some of their impossible magic.

PEOPLE WHO ARE HOT GREEK WAITERS

Once, my sister and I were in a restaurant in Greece, having a fight, and the hot waiter (all waiters in Greece are hot) took one look at our bleak, tear-puffed faces and said, "Ouzo power." He brought us two little glasses of cold, cloudy ouzo, and the ouzo cured our fight. OUZO POWER.

PEOPLE WHO SMILE AT YOU ON THE STREET

It's always nice when any noncreepy stranger smiles at you. There

is not enough interstranger smiling going on these days. I also appreciate it when people working in customer service behave in a genuinely nice manner. Thank you. Please enjoy this large tip for your wonderful smile.

PEOPLE WHO DON'T KNOW HOW TO DRINK

Sometimes a person forgets to eat dinner, or sometimes they just didn't have time or money, and then they end up at the bar and the only snacks available are tallboys. And yes, sure, sometimes they grab your beard and tell you, "You are drinking the most successful sausage," even though that's barely even English, and then they lose their keys and have to sleep on your floor, where they wake up utterly bewildered and have to walk all the way home across town and drink a Big Gulp of Sprite for breakfast on a Thursday. Be kind to these people. They mean well.

PEOPLE WHO ARE ONLY INTERESTING WHEN THEY'RE DRUNK

This one is a bummer, but it's so much less depressing than its half brother, which is People Who Are Just Boring All the Time.

PEOPLE WHO BELIEVE IN SASQUATCH

What's that? You couldn't afford your bunion surgery because you spent all your money on Sasquatch detectors? And now your bunion hurts? Bummer. A few years ago, a friend of mine told me that he'd discovered the secret to finding Sasquatch (he's a believer

because once, in an Idaho forest, he "heard things" that he "couldn't explain") and called some cryptozoological society to announce his epiphany: "Just find out what it eats, and then go to where that is." He and I, we are not friends anymore.

PEOPLE WHO DON'T BELIEVE IN EVOLUTION BUT LOVE ANTIBIOTICS

Seriously? Either you believe in science or you don't. If you want to say sentences to me like "God made the earth 29 years ago out of Billy Graham's stool" or "Every time you take the morning-after pill, Satan has two orgasms," then go ahead and stay away from Dr. Syringey O'Medicine, MD, from here on out. Because you know that pill that made your strep throat go away? Science invented that. For you. Hey, why don't you just pray for God to take care of that root canal? I'll tell you why: Because God didn't go to dental school, because dental schools don't admit people who DON'T EXIST.

WIZARDS

Assholes with beards who do magic. In modern times, wizards look just like normal people, because they've learned to wear tracksuits and tuxedos over their robes. This means that wizards could be anywhere. Can you trust the people you work with not to be wizards?

RUSSIANS

Citizens of Russia. The sworn enemies of wizards.

RUSSIAN WIZARDS

Don't be ridiculous.

PEOPLE WHO LET THEIR CAT WALK ACROSS THEIR KITCHEN CUTTING BOARD, EVEN THOUGH THOSE ARE THE SAME FUCKING PAWS THAT HAVE BEEN TRAMPING AROUND THAT SHIT-FILLED CAT BOX AND I DON'T SEE A KITTY FOOT-WASHING STATION AROUND HERE, DO YOU?

Well? Do you? ANSWER THE QUESTION.

PEOPLE WHO DON'T KNOW HOW TO NAVIGATE A FOUR-WAY STOP OR AN UNCONTROLLED INTERSECTION

Can a lady get a wave, please? Just a courtesy wave. That's all I ask. These people are under the impression that rules do not apply to them. They do not have to wait their turn because they are special. They are probably the worst people on this entire list, and that *includes* wizards.

ANIMALS THAT ARE REALLY PEOPLE WHO GOT TRANSFORMED BY A WITCH

These are people who got on the wrong side of a witch. Now they are turkeys and iguanas or some shit, and all they can do is cry (except

not really, because emotional tears are a physiological phenomenon unique to humans and possibly camels). Don't loan these people money, because they obviously have bad judgment.

PEOPLE WHO THINK "HIPSTERS" ARE A THING

You guys, "hipsters" are not a thing. Put it to bed. PUT IT TO BED.

PEOPLE WHO ARE JUST A DOWN-TO-EARTH GUY, WHO ENJOYS THE LITTLE THINGS IN LIFE LIKE GOING FOR WALKS, LIFTING WEIGHTS, OR JUST DOING WHATEVER (LOL), WHOSE FRIENDS WOULD PROBABLY DESCRIBE HIM AS HONEST, TRUTHFUL, LOYAL, AFFECTIONATE, COMPASSIONATE, AND ROMANCEFUL, AND IS LOOKING FOR A WOMAN WHO IS THAT RARE COMBINATION OF STUNNING ON THE OUTSIDE AND BEAUTIFUL ON THE INSIDE, AND MOST IMPORTANTLY DOWN-TO-EARTH, ENJOYS THE LITTLE THINGS IN LIFE, LOVES CHILDREN, ANIMALS, HAS A PASSION, LAUGHTER. I ESPECIALLY LIKE ASIANS.

Oh shoot, I'm actually busy from now until the moment of my death.

PEOPLE WHO TRY TO PRETEND LIKE THEY ALREADY KNEW THE STORY ABOUT JIMMY STEWART SMUGGLING A YETI HAND OUT OF NEPAL IN HIS WIFE'S UNDERPANTS

I do not believe you, unless your name is Jimmy Stewart's Wife's

Vagina. And I'm pretty sure Jimmy Stewart's Wife's Vagina doesn't know how to read. So . . .

PEOPLE WHO SAY "WHOLE FOODS? MORE LIKE WHOLE PAYCHECK!"

Some people, when talking about the grocery store chain Whole Foods, like to say, "Whole Foods? More like Whole Paycheck!" And when those people say, "Whole Foods? More like Whole Paycheck!" *I* like to say, "Whole Foods? More like Whole Paycheck? More like Whole Foods more like Whole Paycheck more like Whole Still While I Murder You!!!" Because SERIOUSLY, JUST GO TO A DIFFERENT GROCERY STORE IF YOU'RE SO MAD ABOUT IT.

PEOPLE WHO JUST THREW UP IN THEIR MOUTH A LITTLE

No, you didn't, liar. Get a new catchphrase. This one is deceased.

WOMEN

Women are people! Make a note of it! (See also What No One Else Will Tell You About Feminism, page 182.)

AMERICAN PEOPLE OF IRISH DESCENT

Look, Kevin, you're from fucking Fresno, not County Cork, so unless you're about to grant me three wishes or whatever, JUST SHUT. THE FUCK. UP.

PEOPLE WHO ARE BILL PAXTON

I really enjoyed your work in *Twister*.

PEOPLE WHO MISS THE POINT

(See also: People Who Choose to Correct You About the Definition of "Hobo," People Who Claim to Be Afraid of Clowns, People Who Don't Watch TV, People Who Will Just Have a Bite of Whatever You're Having, Old People Who Think Pigeons Are Their Best Friends, People Who Don't Believe in Evolution but Love Antibiotics, People Who Are Bill Paxton, and Babies.)

PEOPLE WHO DON'T MISS THE POINT

I love you.

ACKNOWLEDGMENTS

The authors would like to acknowledge our boss and spirit animal, Tim Keck. Without him, *The Stranger* would not exist and neither would this book. All of the contributors—Grant Brissey, Paul Constant, Goldy, Jen Graves, Jonathan Golob, Eric Grandy, Anthony Hecht, Brendan Kiley, Madeline Macomber, Cienna Madrid, Charles Mudede, David Schmader, Stuart Smithers, and Jesse Vernon—are made out of solid gold. So are *Stranger* staffers Gillian Anderson, Dominic Holden, Anna Minard, Kelly O, Eli Sanders, Dave Segal, and Megan Seling. Hearts! Likewise: Bob Fikso and Laurie Saito were indispensably helpful. Flowers! Also, we heap thanks upon Corianton Hale, who made this book so fucking beautiful, and Whitney Ricketts, Gary Luke, and Sarah Plein, who ushered it out into the world. Kittens! Oh, and especially: Thanks, Mom and Dad. Sorry about all the bad words.

INDEX

A

abortion, 39–40, 104–6, 178, 184
acid, 135
addiction, 130–31, 136–37, 138
adult, how to drink like an, 122–23
AIDS/HIV, 47, 49, 87–89, 111–13
Alaska, 23
alcohol. *See* drinking
Allen, Woody, 7
America, a guide to, 17–24
anal sex, 48, 49, 72–75, 97–98, 111–13
angerbombs, 224
animals that are really people, 239–40
art, majoring in, 6–7

art posters, 170
ask someone out, how to, 29
asshats, 120, 157, 187
Axe body spray, 25

B

babies, 236
banks, 191
bars
    craft cocktail, 126–27
    gay/lesbian, 27, 46, 108
    tipping at, 123, 126, 192–93
bathrooms
    herpes, 62–63
    kink, 92, 93
    sex in, 27, 50
    toilets, 144–46
BDSM, 87–89, 90–93

beer, 124, 192–93
bees, gay, 46
bigots, anti-gay, 42, 43, 45, 47, 66–69, 85–86, 178, 179–81, 196–97
bike, riding a, 192
binge drink, how to, 118–19
biology, majoring in, 9
birth control, 36–37, 104–6, 184
    See also condoms
bisexual people, 27–28, 44–45, 48, 75–77, 79–81, 83–85, 90–91
bison, gay, 46
books. *See* literature; write good, how to
boyfriends. *See* sex and dating
break up, how to, 38, 98–99

245

broken heart, how to get over a, 212–15

"brothas," use of, by white people, 235

C

California, 19–20

car, driving a, 43–44, 124, 192, 239

caribou, gay, 46

Carnot, Sadi, 6

casual sex, how to have, 34

cats, gay, 46

cats, walking across the kitchen cutting board, 239

cheating, 64–66, 69–70, 84, 100–2

cheetahs, gay, 46

chemistry, majoring in, 10

chicken, roasted, 163–65

Christians. *See* Jesus; religion

classical music, majoring in, 10–11

clowns, 233

clubs
likewise-sexual, 28
University Anti-Ugg, 4

cocaine, 132–33

coffee
barista, working as a, 226–27
make your own, 165
Pacific Northwest, 18

college paper, how to write a, 207–8

coming out, 27, 41–45, 85–86

communications, majoring in, 5, 13

compliment, how to take a, 141

computer science, majoring in, 8

computers, how to use, 195–200
See also internet

condoms, 36, 38, 47, 49, 88, 106, 111–13

conversation, how to have a, 140–41

cornography, 197

cover letter, how to write a, 208–10

crack, 132, 225–26

"Crack-Up, The" (Fitzgerald), 202–5, 206, 207

credit cards, eschewing, 189–90

credit unions, 191

crush, turning into something more, 28–29

D

Dalí, Salvador, 7, 170

dating. *See* sex and dating

De Niro, Robert, 7

Democrats, 47, 177–79

diarrhea-hives, 30

dies, when someone you love, 216

DiGiorno, 25

dogs, gay, 46

dolphins, gay, 46

dragons, Komodo, 31

dreams, telling other people about your, 140, 207

drinking, 59–62, 64–66, 115–27, 192–93, 236, 237

driving a car, 43–44, 124, 192, 239

dropping out, 15–16

drugs, 20, 22, 24, 121–22, 129–38, 225–26

drunk, synonyms for, 119

E

economics, majoring in, 12

ecstasy, 134

Einstein, Albert, 6

elephants, gay, 46

employment, 191–92, 217–30, 232

English literature, 5, 11–12, 13, 172–74
See also write good, how to

essence, womanly, 145

evolution, 9, 42, 238

F

Facebook, how NOT to, 198

feminism, 82–83, 84, 182–87

Fermi, Enrico, 6

fetishes. *See* kink

film nerds, flirting with, 171–72

financial advice courtesy of the bible, 189–93

Fitzgerald, F. Scott, 202–5, 206, 207

fog, 12

food

  coffee, make your own, 165

  foodie, how to (not) be a, 153–56

  organic food, 165–66

  recipes, 157–65

  vegetarian, so you're a, 157

foot fetishes, 95–96

forks, 17, 224

Freud, Sigismund Schlomo, 7

friends, making, 4

friends, overdosing, 137

fruit flies, gay, 46

G

Gambit, Mintz-Plasse, 33

Garbage Patch, Great Pacific, 151

gay, how to be, 41–51

  anti-gay bigots, 42, 43, 45, 47, 66–69, 85–86, 178, 179–81, 196–97

  college, where to go to, 45

  coming out, 27, 41–45, 85–86

guide to America, 19, 21

history of gay people, 46–47

Savage Love, 66–69, 70–72, 85–86, 87–90, 91–93, 95–98, 111–13

sex with a man if you're a man, 48–49

sex with a woman if you're a woman, 50–51

sleeping with straight people, 47–48

gender is a social construct, 185–86

genitals, photography of, 198–99

gentry, landed, 26

Gere, Richard, 3

girlfriends. *See* sex and dating

girls. *See entries under lady*

Golden Rule and beer, 192–93

Google, 43, 187

Greek waiters, hot, 236

Gruyère, 162–63, 227

guest at a party, how to be a, 141–42

H

hands, pee-, 146

hangover, how to deal with a, 116–18

Hawaii, 23–24

heartbreak, 38, 98–99, 211–16

heroin, 136–37

"hipsters," 240

history, majoring in, 13–14

HIV/AIDS, 47, 49, 87–89, 111–13

hoboes, 26, 231–32

honesty, 35, 44–45

housewives, 184

I

infidelity, 64–66, 69–70, 84, 100–2

internet

  anti-gay bigots, 43, 196–97

  computer science, majoring in, 8

  Facebook, how NOT to, 198

  genitals, emailing pictures of, 198–99

  male privilege, 187

  online dating, 98–99, 108, 199–200

  porn, 8, 198

  spam, 199

  things it is good for, 195–96

  things it is not good for, 196

  trolls, 196–97

Irish people, 241

J

Jesus, 178, 179–81, 192

jobs, 191–92, 217–30, 232

jocks, shock, 3
journalism, majoring in, 5, 12–13

K
Kafka, 54, 117
killer whales, gay, 46
kink, 86–96
kiss, how to, 30–31

L
lady-areas, 37, 187
lady-brains, 5
lady-parts, 50, 187
lady-people, 34, 36–37, 82–83, 84, 140–41, 145, 182–87, 241
  See also abortion; rape
laundry, how to do, 147–52
lesbians. *See* gay, how to be
lights, black, 3
lions, gay, 46
literature, 5, 11–12, 13, 172–74
  See also write good, how to
lizards, gay, 46
LSD, 135

M
macaroni and cheese, 161–63
majors, 3
  everything there is to know about, 6–15

you should not major in, 5
manners, 139–46
marijuana, 20, 131–32
masturbation, 50, 82–83, 196, 197
men-people, 182
mermaid, evil, 165
meth, 22, 133–34
Midwest, 19, 45
Mintz-Plasse Gambit, 33
monks, 10
moths, gay, 46
Mountains, 22
movie nerds, flirting with, 171–72
mushrooms, 135–36
music, 10–11, 167–70
mustaches, 2

N
narratives, master, the death of, 12
Nazis, 15
needle play, 89–90
Newton, Isaac, 6
Northeast, 21–22

O
old people, 20, 235
one-night stand, how to have a, 33
online dating, 98–99, 108, 199–200
oral sex, 49, 69–70
organic food, 165–66

ouzo power, 236
overdosing, 137

P
Pacific Northwest, 18
parents, 44, 82–86
party, how to be a guest at a, 141–42
party, how to host a, 142–44
pasta, 160–61
Paxton, Bill, 242
penguins, gay, 46
people
  different from you, how to get along with, 1–2
  different kinds of, 231–42
  fat, 196
  friends, making, 4
  roommates, how to get along with, 3–4
  See also lady-people; manners; religion; sex and dating
philosophy, majoring in, 5, 14–15
physics, majoring in, 6
pigeon love, 235
poetry, 11, 210
politics, 46–47, 175–87
polyamory, 75–82
ponies, lathered, 125
porn, 8, 84–85, 184, 198
positions you need to try, sexual, 32–33

power, ouzo, 236

pregnancy. *See* abortion; birth control

professor, how to sleep with your, 53–57

psychology, majoring in, 7

R

raccoons, gay, 46

rape, 102–4, 183–84, 185

recipes, 157–65

relationships. *See* sex and dating

religion, 22, 39

anti-gay bigots, 42, 43, 45, 66–69, 178, 179–81

different kinds of people, 238

financial advice courtesy of the bible, 189–93

politics, 178, 179–81

Savage Love, 66–72

Republicans, 47, 177–79

restaurants

foodie, how to (not) be a, 153–56

working in, 191–92, 217–30

romantic date, how to take someone on a, 30

roofied, how to get, 121–22

roommates, 3–4, 59–66

rosé, 125

Russians, 239

S

Sasquatch, 18, 237–38

Savage Love, 59–113

seagulls, gay, 46

sentences, a close read of, 203–5

sex and dating, 25–40

abortion, 39–40, 104–6, 178, 184

anal sex, 48, 49, 72–75, 97–98, 111–13

ask someone out, how to, 29

biology, majoring in, 9

birth control, 36–37, 104–6, 184

bisexual people, 27–28, 44 45, 48, 75–77, 79–81, 83–85, 90–91

break up, how to, 38, 98–99

broken heart, how to get over a, 212–15

casual sex, how to have, 34

cheating, 64–66, 69–70, 84, 100–2

condoms, 36, 38, 47, 49, 88, 106, 111–13

crush, how to turn into something more, 28–29

genitals, photography of, 198–99

get with a bi/trans/differently sexual person if you are a bi/trans/differently sexual per-

son, how to, 27–28

get with a boy if you are a girl, how to, 25

get with a gay/lesbian if you are a gay/lesbian, how to, 27

get with a girl if you are a boy, how to, 25–26

honesty, 35, 44–45

kink, 86–96

kiss, how to, 30–31

one-night stand, how to have a, 33

online dating, 98–99, 108, 199–200

parents, 44, 82–86

people, different kinds of, 236, 240

polyamory, 75–82

porn, 8, 84–85, 184, 198

professor, how to sleep with your, 53–57

put your parts in or on another person, how to successfully, 31–32

rape, 102–4, 183–84, 185

relationship, how to be in a, 35

romantic date, how to take someone on a, 30

roommates, 59–66

Savage Love, 59–113

sexual positions you need to try, 32–33

STIs, 36–38, 47, 48–49, 62–63, 87–90, 111–13

trans people, 27–28, 106–9
virgins, 109–13
See also gay, how to be
sexually transmitted infections (STIs), 36–38, 47, 48–49, 62–63, 87–90, 111–13
sheep, crazy sand-, 20
shitheels, 126, 215
slugs, cave-, 31
slut-shaming, 185
smiling, interstranger, 236–37
soup, 157–58
South, 21, 45
Southwest, 20, 45
spam, 199
spoons, 32, 224
spying on your roommate, 63–64
stairs, falling down, 207, 233
Stewart, Jimmy, 240–41
STIs. *See* sexually transmitted infections (STIs)
submission. *See* BDSM
sugar babies, 87–89
suicide, 9, 216

T
tacos, 158–59
talk to people, how to, 140–41
tattooing yourself, 179
teacher, how to sleep with your, 53–57
television, 233–34
Texans, shaky, 3–4
theater, majoring in, 8–9
threesomes. *See* polyamory
throwing up, 120–21
tipping
  bars, 123, 126, 192–93
  restaurants, 155, 223–24
toilets, 62–63, 92, 93, 144–46
trans people, 27–28, 106–9
trees, sex with, 86–87
trolls, 196–97
turtles, gay, 46
TV, 233–34
Twitter, how to, 197

U
Uggs, 3, 4
unicorns, liquid, 126

V
vaginal sex, 69–70, 110–11
vegetarians, 157
velociraptors, 115
videotaping your roommate, 63–64
virgins, 109–13
vomiting, 120–21
voting, 176–77, 183

W
Warhol, Andy, 7
wash your clothes, how to, 151–52
whimsy, 234
Whole Foods, 241
wine, the deal with, 124–25
witches, 239–40
wizards, 238, 239
women. *See entries under lady*
write good, how to, 201–10

Z
Zork, 8

ABOUT THE AUTHORS

LINDY WEST writes about movies, movie stars, exclamation points, lady stuff, large frightening fish, and more. You may have witnessed her single-handedly putting an end to the *Sex and the City* movie series. Lindy's work also appears in *GQ*, *New York* magazine, the *Daily Telegraph*, the *Guardian*, the *New York Daily News*, Deadspin, and other places. She is a staff writer for Jezebel.com.

DAN SAVAGE writes the sex-and-relationship advice column "Savage Love." He is also the founder of the It Gets Better Project and the editorial director of *The Stranger*.

CHRISTOPHER FRIZZELLE joined *The Stranger* as the books editor in 2003 and has been editor-in-chief since 2007. He has written about hunting for magic mushrooms in the wild, the effect of 9/11 on his military family, and creepy old buildings, among other topics. He hosts a regular silent-reading party in a hotel lobby.

BETHANY JEAN CLEMENT writes about eating food, knowing cows (and eating them), drinking drinks, and more. Her work has appeared in the *Best Food Writing* anthologies, *Food & Wine*, *Town & Country*, Gourmet.com, *Beard House*, the Greenwood Space Travel Supply Co., and elsewhere. She is the managing editor of *The Stranger*.

A NOTE ON THE TYPE

BY CORIANTON HALE

The body of this book was lovingly set in Century Expanded because all of us at *The Stranger* think it's beautiful, and because Bethany suggested it in a really sweet, convincing way. It's based on Century Roman, cut in 1894 by Linn Boyd Benton (a commission for *Century Magazine*) and retooled by his son Morris Fuller Benton in 1900. It also marks M. F. Benton's invention of the "type family," a group of fonts that adhere to a similar feeling but offer individual variations. Benton went on to invent the xylophone, cuticle cream, and "jazz hands." I like his work on Century Expanded the best because it's incredibly practical, but full of stylish details, earning its use from bibles to magazines, tetherballs to tombstones. It is also the magical body font we use in *The Stranger* itself, which makes you believe what we are saying is true and well-researched.